'I welcome the publication of this volume which contains most salient issues that need to be considered when discussing the contributions of AU peace operations to the maintenance of international peace and security. The dynamics around the international support for African peace operations provide both opportunities and challenges which need to be pragmatically scrutinized as has been done in this volume.

I therefore highly recommend this volume to readers that are interested in gaining a deeper understanding of the issues and challenges involved in contemporary AU-UN support arrangements.'

Ambassador Boubacar G. Diarra

'In all, this is a valuable contribution to the emerging body of knowledge on inter-organisational cooperative arrangements in Peace Operations.'

Markus Derblom, Head, Department for Peace Support Operations, FOI

SUPPORTING AFRICAN PEACE OPERATIONS

Edited by

Linnéa Gelot, Ludwig Gelot and Cedric de Coning

The Nordic Africa Institute
Dag Hammarskjöld Foundation
Norwegian Institute of International Affairs
2012

NAI Policy Dialogue is a series of short reports on policy relevant issues concerning Africa today. Aimed at professionals working within aid agencies, ministries of foreign affairs, NGOs and media, these reports aim to inform the public debate and to generate input in the sphere of policymaking. The writers are researchers and scholars engaged in African issues from several disciplinary points of departure. Most have an institutional connection to the Nordic Africa Institute or its research networks. The reports are internally endorsed and reviewed externally.

Indexing terms
Africa
Civil war
Conflicts
Peace corps
Peacebuilding
Peacekeeping
International cooperation
International security

*The opinions expressed in this volume are those of the authors
and do not necessarily reflect the views of Nordiska Afrikainsitutet.*

Language checking: Peter Colenbrander
Front Cover: Stuart Price / AU-UN IST Photo
UN-AU Support: A Ugandan medical officer serving with the African Union Mission in Somalia (AMISOM) walks past a tent at the mission's Level II field hospital at the operation's headquarters in Mogadishu, Somalia.
Photos of the seminar participants: Jean-Philippe Deschamps-Laporte
ISSN 1654-6709
ISBN 978-91-7106-723-4
© The authors and Nordiska Afrikainstitutet 2012
Production: Byrå4
Print on demand, Lightning Source UK Ltd.

Contents

Glossary

AMIB	AU Mission in Burundi
AMIS	AU Mission in Darfur
AMISOM	AU Mission in Somalia
APSA	AU Peace and Security Architecture
ASF	African Standby Force
AU	African Union
AUPSC	AU Peace and Security Council
AUPSOD	AU Peace Support Operations Division
BINUB	UN Integrated Office in Burundi
DFS	Dept of Field Services (UN)
DHF	Dag Hammarskjöld Foundation
DPKO	Dept of Peacekeeping Operations (UN)
DRC	Democratic Republic of Congo
ECCAS	Economic Community of Central African States
ECOMOG	ECOWAS Monitoring Group
ECOWAS	Economic Community of West African States
EU	European Union
IDP	Internally Displaced Person
JEM	Justice and Equality Movement
LJM	Liberation and Justice Movement (Darfur)
NAI	Nordic Africa Institute
NUPI	Norwegian Institute for International Affairs
OAU	Organisation of African Unity
ONUB	UN Operation in Burundi
P5	Permanent UNSC members
PCC	Police Contributing Country
RDL	Rally for Democracy and Liberty
REC	Regional Economic Community
RUF	Revolutionary United Front (Sierra Leone)
SADC	Southern African Development Community
SLM/A	Sudan Liberation Movement/Army
SPLM	Sudan People's Liberation Movement
TCC	Troop Contributing Country
UN	United Nations
UNAMID	AU-UN Hybrid Mission in Darfur
UNAMSIL	UN Mission in Sierra Leone
UNGA	UN General Assembly

UNMIL	UN Mission in Liberia
UNOAU	UN Office to the AU
UNOCI	UN Operation in Côte d'Ivoire
UNOMIL	UN Observer Mission in Liberia
UNMIS	UN Mission in Sudan
UNOMSIL	UN Observer Force in Sierra Leone
UNSC	UN Security Council
UNSOA	UN Support Office for Amisom

Foreword

Since the early 1990s, African regional and sub-regional organisations such as the African Union and its predecessor the OAU, ECOWAS and SADC have shown increasing willingness and capacity to deploy peace operations on the continent. The 1994 Rwandan genocide, and the inability of the UNSC to respond to the crisis in timely fashion, strengthened the resolve of the then OAU and its successor to develop its own capacity to deal with such crises in future. However, Africa is home to the bulk of the world's least developed countries, and even the most prosperous countries in Africa are still struggling with huge development backlogs. It is thus not surprising that the AU and sub-regional organisations like ECOWAS, SADC and ECCAS face serious financial and logistical challenges in deploying and sustaining their own peace support operations.

At the same time, the UN is already overstretched, with approximately 120,000 military, police and civilian peacekeepers deployed and a budget of almost US$ 8 billion per year. In addition, its unique form of post-conflict peacekeeping, which requires a ceasefire agreement in place and the prior consent of the parties to the conflict, means that it has been unable to respond to some of the most serious conflicts in Africa, such as those in Rwanda, Darfur and Somalia. This has resulted in a new awareness that the international peace and security system requires a network of actors with a broad set of capacities, so that regional organisations can undertake peace operations in situations where the UN is unable to do so. However, given the weak economic base of the African continent, the AU and sub-regional organisations need external resources to be able to deploy and sustain peace support operations.

This is why the topic of support models for African peace operations has become so important. We now have almost two decades of experience to consider, and various different models, such as direct donor support to the AU and troop contributing countries during the AU Mission in Darfur, the various UN support packages to this mission and the subsequent joint AU-UN Hybrid Mission in Darfur, and the current AU Mission in Somalia that is supported by a dedicated UN support mission, as well by the EU and other donors. It is unlikely that Somalia will be the last AU mission that requires some form of international support. It thus makes sense to reflect on these models to assess their strengths and weaknesses, and to consider what lessons and best practices we can extract from these experiences for the future.

This is why the AU welcomed the initiative by the Nordic Africa Institute, the Dag Hammarskjöld Foundation and the Norwegian Institute for International Affairs to convene a seminar on this topic in Uppsala, Sweden, on 15 and 16 December 2011. The AU hopes that this report will serve as the basis for further reflection, and that it will contribute to improved partnership modalities between the AU and its strategic partners in future peace operations.

Sivuyile Bam
Head: Peace Support Operations Department
African Union Commission

Acknowledgements

The Nordic Africa Institute, the Dag Hammarskjöld Foundation and the Norwegian Institute for International Affairs convened a seminar in Uppsala, Sweden, on 15 and 16 December 2011, that gathered together AU, EU and UN officials closely involved in peace operations in Africa with a view to comparing their experiences with the different support models that have been used to date in Sudan and Somalia. The seminar was primarily funded by the Swedish International Development Agency (SIDA), through NAI, but both DHF and NUPI made important contributions as well. The NUPI contribution was supported by the Norwegian ministry of foreign affairs under the auspices of the Training for Peace in Africa Programme.

This edited volume is based on the seminar in Uppsala, and serves as a report of the proceedings. Most of the chapters are based on papers delivered at the seminar, and the introductory and concluding chapters serve to provide context, analysis and commentary on the papers, based in large part on the discussions that took place during the seminar. The seminar was organised under the Chatham House formula, which allows participants, most of whom were current officers of the AU, EU and UN, to contribute freely without quotes being attributed to any individual. This edited volume is thus not the type of report of proceedings that attempts to faithfully summarise what was said at the seminar. Instead, it aims to capture the most salient issues concerning the topic. While it is based on and guided by the presentations to and discussions at the seminar in Uppsala, it also goes beyond by engaging with the broader literature and debates on the topic.

We wish to thank the participants for their candid comments and engagement and for the paper contributions we received. We would like to extend our thanks to the executive directors of the NAI, NUPI and the DHF. Special thanks go to the NAI administration and research support staff, and in particular to Ingrid Andersson. Additionally, we gratefully acknowledge the comments and suggestions of an anonymous reviewer.

The editors

Executive Summary

Over the last decade the AU has deployed three peace operations in Burundi (AMIB), Darfur (AMIS) and Somalia (AMISOM).[1] In each of these cases, the AU made a significant contribution to stabilising the situation. In Burundi, AMIB contributed to the transition from a fragile ceasefire involving only one party to a comprehensive peace agreement, and the operation was handed over to the UN (ONUB). In Darfur, the AU made a contribution to protecting those people where it had a presence, for example around IDP camps, and when the international community decided to further scale-up the mission it became the first ever AU-UN hybrid peacekeeping operation (UNAMID). In Somalia, the AU first created a pocket of stability around the government sector in Mogadishu and then increased the areas under its control until they included most of greater Mogadishu. With the entry of Kenya in the south, and with the integration of the Kenyan forces into AMISOM, the mission is now able to expand its stabilising influence over an even larger part of Somalia. However, sustainable peace is elusive and dependent on a political process.

Especially in Darfur and Somalia, the AU has been requested by the international community to take on the peace operations role because it was the only organisation with the political credibility and the peace operations capability to do so. And in these cases, the international community was willing to provide financial and material support to enable the AU to undertake these operations on its behalf. However, while the AU has become an important peace operations actor on the African continent, one of the most significant characteristics of its peace operations is its reliance on international assistance. Africa is home to most of the least developed countries in the world, and even its most developed nations face severe development backlogs. Africa's ability to finance and support its peace operations is thus limited.

As a result, international support for AU peace operations is an important factor. Without it, the AU would not be able to make the contribution to the maintenance of international peace and security that is has been able to make in Burundi, Darfur and Somalia. The dynamics of international support for African peace operations raise a number of opportunities and challenges. Such support can lead to close cooperation between the AU, the UN, the EU and other funding partners. However, this relationship can also, if not well managed, easily deteriorate into a donor-beneficiary relationship.

One major challenge is that the AU's ability to independently choose the

---

1 As well as various types of peace operations in the Comoros in 2004 and 2007–08.

missions it may wish to engage in, and the scope of that engagement, is significantly constrained by its dependency on others to fund and support its missions. Unilateral decisions by its partners to not support a mission that the AU wants to become involved in, such as Libya in 2011, or not to support it on a scale the AU may believe necessary, for instance, Somalia in 2011, severely constrain the AU. This means that in reality it can only deploy and maintain peace operations with the consent of its international partners. In consequence, the nature of the relationship between the AU and its partners is critical to the success of African peace operations.

The actual models used to finance and support AU peace operations have been different in each of the three AU operations to date. AMIB was largely self-financed in that the lead nation, South Africa, had to assume responsibility for the bulk of the costs. The United Kingdom and the United States supported the contingents from Ethiopia and Mozambique that complemented the mission. In Darfur, a large and complex constellation of partners supported the mission. The EU provided the bulk of the support, but many other partners contributed enabling support or contracted directly with service providers. When the AU mission was re-hatted as an AU-UN hybrid mission, the budget increased fourfold and funding and support was provided by the UN-assessed contribution financing mechanism and the UN's mission support system. In Somalia, the mission started out using the direct donor support model developed for AMIS, but then transitioned into a new form of support whereby a UN support mission is deployed alongside AMISOM and the UN assessed contribution budget is used to support certain aspects of the AU mission. In addition, the mission is also supported by the EU and donors. The EU provides, among other things, the allowances for the soldiers. Other donors provide in-kind support, for instance by providing military equipment and training to TCCs.[2]

A number of support models have thus been attempted and have evolved over this period, and all the parties engaged in this process has shown much flexibility and innovation in working around problems and finding solutions for the myriad challenges such operations generate. Some have criticised this process for its *ad hoc* nature and piecemeal approach, but others have commented that it is impossible to plan too far ahead in relation to highly dynamic and complex situations, and argue that one has to take an evolutionary

---

2   ECOWAS-AU-UN collaboration in Côte d'Ivoire (various missions from 2003 onwards) may also be worth assessing in relation to support models and hybrid peace operations. This seminar did not look in-depth at that case.

approach in such circumstances. Whilst these models clearly show significant evolution and learning over the years since the first operation was deployed in Burundi in 2004, the fact remains that all these missions also faced severe challenges, and that a major factor was lack of resources, equipment and critical support services. The evolution of these models can thus be commended, but one can at the same time identify significant gaps between, for instance, the level of support available for AU operations and the level of support that standard UN operations enjoy.

At the seminar convened by NAI, DHF and NUPI in Uppsala, Sweden on 15 and 16 December 2011, AU, EU and UN officials closely involved in these operations were gathered together with a view to comparing experiences with the different support models that have been used to date in Sudan and Somalia. The aim of the seminar was to identify lessons from these experiences and to generate policy-relevant knowledge that can improve the way the AU and its partners manage their relationship, including the support aspect, in future.

This report consists of some of the papers presented at the seminar, as well as general commentary and observations. It is not a verbatim report of proceedings, but instead attempts to reflect the rich discussions that took place in Uppsala with a view to sharing the most pertinent insights more widely.

The participants agreed that the relationship between the AU and other key stakeholders such as the UN, EU and most donor countries is of particular importance for peace operations in Africa. This relationship is unfortunately complicated by the fact that the AU is not only a major peace operations actor, but is also engaged in various partnerships aimed at building its own capacity, including its peace operations capacity. The AU thus has to simultaneously manage several relationships with the same partners, ranging from a donor-recipient relationship in some circumstances to an equal, if not leading, partner in others. These factors make these relationships extremely complicated and sensitive. Tension and frustration can easily arise in such a delicate arrangement, and the seminar touched on several examples where developments on the ground did indeed result in such tensions and frustrations.

In fact, given the magnitude of the challenges and the scale of the undertakings, involving thousands of personnel and millions of dollars, and given the loss of life of the peacekeepers and the people they have been deployed to protect, one cannot but be astonished that these relationships have by and large been sustained and strengthened over the period under analysis. This indicates that despite the very real challenges, all the parties accept and recognise that the role of the AU is critical, and that its relationships with the UN, EU and other partners, however difficult, need to be maintained, improved, strengthened and further refined. All stakeholders are thus committed to make the relationships work.

At the same time, there are various factors that detract from the overall constructive nature of the relationships. Seminar participants identified as major negative factors the AU Commission's lack of capacity, insufficient political commitment by African member states and the short-term and self-interested motives of some of the partners. Some participants also stressed that UNSC permanent members need to value and ensure better coordination of AU-UN positions in response to conflict in Africa for the sake of their own legitimacy and the sake of the efficiency and success of the operations the UNSC authorises. Although the AU Commission has done much over the last decade to clarify its policies and guidelines towards peace operations, and to improve its internal capacity to plan and manage peace operations, seminar participants agreed that the AU's capacity in this regard is still lacking in several significant areas. This undermines both the relationship between the AU and its partners and the AU's ability to exercise effective command and control over its own missions.

The second factor is the level of political engagement by African member states in AU peace operations. Even the members of the AUPSC seem to accept the significant influence of the UN, EU and major donors on AU peace operations, and seem to be willing to cede the initiative and leadership of missions to partners. African member states need to significantly increase their political commitment to and engagement with the AU Commission and AU peace operations before the AU Commission will have the backing and impetus needed to develop its internal capacity. Another significant factor is the willingness of African countries to contribute to the AU Peace Fund, and to otherwise contribute financially and in kind to AU peace operations. Too often, African member states seem content to sit back and let international partners take financial responsibility for the AU's peace efforts. The AU's partners have no incentive to increase support for African peace operations beyond the bare minimum if African member states do not significantly upscale their own political and financial support to African peace operations.

The third factor is the short-termism and self-interest of the AU's partners. While these partners are strategically committed to support the AU and to help achieve the mission goals together with the AU, several bureaucratic and political tendencies undermine this strategic consensus. Goals may be strategic and long-term, but funds have to be spent and reported in short-term cycles. This results in short-term, good-enough solutions that may resolve or circumvent immediate challenges, but end up undermining long-term goals, such as when a partner contracts directly with a critical service provider because the AU does not have its own capacity to manage such mission-support contracts. Often such actions end-up substituting whatever limited AU capacity may have. More needs to be done to ensure that most international support also has a capacity-building effect.

Another concern is that international support for AU peace operations seems to be at a level just sufficient to keep the AU peace operation in place, but not for it to be able to achieve its mandate. Financial austerity drives partners to provide the AU missions with as little support as possible. This means that AU missions may be on the ground, which is sufficient for the international community to feel that the problem is being dealt with, but may not have the means to pursue the mission mandate. Partners may thus be motivated by the need to show their electorates and international counterparts that they are doing something to address a particular problem, but may not be committed enough to invest sufficient resources to ensure the success of AU peace operations. This contributes to a self-fulfilling perception that AU peace operations have less capacity and operate at a lower standard than UN peace operations. Even AU member states that also contribute to UN peace operations complain about the different level of support provided their troops serving in an AU operation.

The fourth factor is that too often in the past, UNSC decisions about how to stabilise parts of Africa have led to negative perceptions among the AU as well as some African leaders and parties to conflicts. The UNSC is too often seen as dictating 'Western' or big power priorities and treating the AU as less capable, knowledgeable and professional. Seminar participants agreed on the importance of a shared strategic vision among the AU, UN, EU and the AU's other partners. The lack of such shared vision has negatively impacted the international consensus, the sustainability of funding mechanisms, the effectiveness of AU-UN synergy and the achievement of agreed standards in peace operations.

All these factors are, of course, related. For instance, for capacity building to be effective the AU needs to increase its absorptive capacity. That will not happen until AU member states increase their engagement with African peace operations and enable the AU Commission to develop the required capacity. The same is true of the level of support for and standards of AU peace operations: upliftment of standards will only occur when AU member states are engaged enough to generate the political will necessary for such upliftment. And this is unlikely to happen until African member states increase their own investment in preparing and supporting the soldiers, police offi-

cers and civilians they contribute to AU peace operations, and until they contribute more significantly to the AU Peace Fund and AU peace operations.

Seminar participants also agreed that there is no one optimal support model for AU peace operations. The AU and its partners should avoid trapping themselves in a model that may have evolved to meet the needs of the last mission, but may be wholly inappropriate to the next. The most important lesson seems to be that support models must be flexible and context specific. However, this does not mean that the wheel needs to be reinvented every time a new mission is needed. There are many things the AU and its partners can do to prepare themselves for future support relationships that are flexible and context specific.

The AU and its partners need to establish predictable and dependable mechanisms to ensure they are in regular contact with one another to discuss and guide their peace operation partnerships. Such collaboration systems will not only serve to build greater understanding and trust between partners, but will greatly facilitate interaction when they do need to respond to sudden emergencies, or to deal with situations that generate tensions and frustration among partners.

The AU and its partners will be locked into a mutually dependent relationship for the foreseeable future, and one of the key characteristics of this relationship is the AU's dependence on these partners for mission support. At the same time, partners are dependent on the AU for political credibility, context-specific knowhow and its ability to mount robust stability operations in contexts where no other parties can effectively operate. This mutual dependency forms a solid basis for further strengthening the relationship between them, including further refining and improving stakeholder understanding of how best to support future AU peace operations.

1. Contextualising Support Models for African Peace Operations

Linnéa Gelot, Ludwig Gelot and Cedric de Coning

Introduction

In contemporary peace operations, it is rare that one organisation, such as the UN or AU, will be the sole international actor in any given theatre. In fact, in most cases where there is an international peace operation deployed in Africa, it is likely there will be some form of UN, AU and EU presence. In many cases there would also be several special envoys from interested countries and most likely also from the relevant sub-regional organisation. With so many stakeholders and actors deployed or otherwise engaged in the same country or region, cooperation and coordination become a major consideration.

In this broader context, the relationship between the AU and other key stakeholders such as the UN, EU and most donor countries is of particular importance in Africa. This relationship is complicated by the fact that the AU is not only the primary regional organisation in Africa, but is also engaged in various partnerships aimed at building its own capacity and to carry out its responsibilities. This is especially the case when it comes to AU peace operations. The AU has played a critical role in several such operations, deploying when no other organisations were able or willing to do so. The African continent is home to the bulk of the world's least developed countries, so it is not surprising that the AU lacks the economic base to finance its own peace operations on the continent. Various support models have developed over the years to sustain AU operations.

Given the importance of AU-UN support arrangements for African stability and international peace and security, this report aims to address the following key questions:

- What can be learnt from the opportunities and challenges of previously developed support models?
- What shaped the emergence of these models?
- What are the financial, political, organisational and capacity challenges encountered by partners in establishing support models?

- How does the relationship and emerging partnership between the AU and UN affect the evolution of support models?
- How do AU member states and the UN affect the evolution of support models?

Challenges of Peace Operations in Africa

The challenges that AU, EU and UN peace operations face in Africa arise from three main factors: the diversity of conflicts in Africa; the 'capacity crisis'; and the different peace operational cultures of the organisations that actively deploy missions in Africa.

Conflicts in Africa are as diverse in background, conditions and conflict drivers as they are in their dynamics, consequences and amenability to resolution. Political violence must be understood through a combination of historical and structural features, and elite survival. Conflicts in Africa have at once a transnational and regional character; they are spurred on by international and global factors; and state capacity to provide security and stability to its citizens can differ hugely. The largest and most expensive current UN peace operations are those deployed in Darfur (UNAMID), South Sudan (UNMISS) and in the DRC (MONUSCO). All three are among the most complex scenarios faced by the UN today. In these missions, the peacekeepers have operated amid ongoing conflict, and they have been asked to protect civilians and provide stability, often without adequate capabilities (strategic airlift, utility and tactical helicopters, mobile infantry, etc.). The peacekeepers have had to carry out their tasks in a situation where the political process is weak, stalled or simply absent, and often with limited or declining consent from key parties on the ground (de Coning and Lotze 2010:109).

We use the term 'peace operations', since many of the UN's contemporary missions cannot be adequately captured by the term 'peacekeeping', which suggests that there is a peace agreement or ceasefire in place that the mission is helping to monitor and implement. Peace operations include everything from low intensity peacekeeping operations, such as unarmed or lightly armed military observer missions, to high intensity peace enforcement operations. The protection of civilians, 'robust operations' and the peacebuilding tasks performed during the course of peace operations present particular challenges to the UN peacekeeping enterprise. In the debates about strengthening and improving the this enterprise, the Department of Peacekeeping Operations and the Department of Field Support have emphasised the mismatch between the scale and complexity of peace operations today and existing capabilities

(UN DPKO 2009:20). The diversity of mission mandates and the scope of operations have overstretched the UN's capacity and put enormous pressure on the organisation to meet the expectations of improved stability and peace consolidation that come with the deployment of UN peace operations. In December 2011, the UN had over 119,000 deployed personnel across 15 missions around the world. The budget has soared to almost US$8 billion a year. This creates a significant credibility challenge for UN peace operations.

Historically, most UN missions in Africa have deployed to intra-state conflicts involving varying degrees of internationalisation. These conflicts have proven to be very difficult to transcend, and in most cases the countries remain in transition, fragile and at risk of relapse into violent conflict. In fact, countries such as the Democratic Republic of Congo, Liberia and Sierra Leone have relapsed into violent conflict after or during the deployment of a UN peace operation. Initial post-Cold War UN missions in Namibia and Mozambique were perceived as relative successes, yet they were the exception. They went beyond traditional peacekeeping operations, but only in scope and comprehensiveness. They were still established on the basis of peace agreements, and they still operated according to the UN's three core peacekeeping principles: neutrality, impartiality and the use of force only in self-defence.

The experiences of the United States and the UN in Somalia (the US-led Unified Task Force – UNITAF – in 1992-93 and its successor UN operation in Somalia, UNOSOM II in 1993-95), as symbolised by the 'Black Hawk Down' debacle in Mogadishu, resulted in increased wariness in many Western countries about contributing their own troops to UN peace operations in Africa's civil wars. As an alternative to direct intervention or to contributing troops to UN peace operations, the US and other leading Western countries opted to invest in building the capacity of African countries and African regional organisations to manage their own conflicts (de Coning 2010a:8).

The five permanent UNSC members (P5) were not only unwilling to involve themselves in some of the most deadly African civil wars, they also limited the involvement of the UN in Southern Sudan, the DRC, Liberia, Rwanda and Sierra Leone. This was in part because these civil wars raised the prospect of peace enforcement, and the prevalent view in UN circles at the time was that 'pre-conditions for success' of peace operations included the consent of the warring parties (at a minimum, host state consent), commitment to a comprehensive peace agreement (peace to keep), a clear mandate with a specified end-state and international support. UNSC members unwilling to intervene justified their position on the grounds that all of those preconditions were not in place. Other significant reasons were that they had no direct strategic or economic interest in Africa that could justify taking risks with their own soldiers or taxpayers' money, or that they wanted to avoid clashing with other P5 members over influence in former colonies or countries that were aligned with either side during the Cold War (UNGA-UNSC 2000:§ 105).

Background to African-UN Joint Missions

As pointed out by Abdallah and Aning in this volume, the UN-ECOWAS co-deployment in Liberia in 1993 – the UN Observer Mission in Liberia – was the first experiment in joint peace operations. The pattern of UN-ECOWAS collaboration continued in Sierra Leone when the UN deployed a UN Observer Force in Sierra Leone alongside ECOMOG forces in 1998. These West African examples, and what was learned from these experiments and developments, have helped to situate the current debate about improving support models for African peace operations.

ECOWAS deployed troops to Liberia and Sierra Leone without prior UNSC authorisation, and both engagements quickly evolved into peace enforcement missions. Had a formal UN-ECOWAS relationship already existed, such actions would have presented serious challenges for the UNSC's political control. The UNSC chose to retroactively endorse the operations in Liberia in 1990 and Sierra Leone in 1997 and took on a 'partner' role, yet its monitoring attempts were unconvincing. UNOMIL was a small and unarmed mission co-deployed alongside the ECOMOG force, and dependent for protection on the very force it was meant to monitor.

The UN's involvement in Sierra Leone and Côte d'Ivoire were variants of support missions, not viable in themselves but reliant on ECOMOG's continued presence for their functioning. It could be said that the UNSC 'by default' permitted ECOWAS's peace enforcement actions. The UNSC welcomed regional engagement in these two conflicts where it did not wish to intervene itself from the outset. The Liberian government had sought UN involvement in June 1990, but the UNSC declined. ECOMOG had been deployed in Liberia for two years when the UNSC passed its first resolution on the conflict. In Sierra Leone, the UNSC adopted a policy of 'malign neglect' towards the conflict between 1991 and 1999 (Adebajo 2008: 486). These two examples sparked lively debates among legal specialists on how far these violations of UN Charter Article 2(4) set precedents that threatened this foundational rule (whether a 'customary right' of unauthorised humanitarian intervention can be said to exist). Nigeria launched its Liberia and Sierra Leone interventions in breach of both international law and internal ECOWAS rules (Coleman 2007:77). It is worth noting that the trend continued with the later SADC intervention in Lesotho, and the AU Mission in Burundi. AMIB had been authorised by the UNSC, but on the ground the mission carried out enforcement activities that can be said to have exceeded its mandate.

In terms of capacity and logistical and financial support, the West African examples showed the need for more predictable and sustainable support structures. The costs of ECOWAS peace enforcement operations were largely borne by the lead-state, Nigeria. Similarly, the cost of AMIB was largely borne by South Africa. ECOMOG troops were deployed to Liberia and Sierra Leone without arrangements being in place for logistics and finances. There were around 10,000 troops at the height of each mission in Liberia and Sierra Leone. Several ECOWAS members declined to contribute, in part because their financial and logistical needs could not be met. When the UN deployed UNMIL, it was largely as an attempt to replace ECOWAS with a more independent, neutral mission that had the mandate and the financial and military capacity to bring peace.

First, the West African and AMIB precedents showed that some African states would shoulder financial and military costs if their strategic or national interests were at stake. The most dramatic and/or best equipped interventions in Africa have been dominated by states that had important interests in the particular target state (Herbst 2000:28). One explanation for why Nigeria, for example, wanted to act through ECOWAS was to increase the international and African legitimacy of the missions. However, Nigeria never managed to shake off accusations that it was a biased intervener interested in a certain political development in its neighbourhood. Hence, its interventions were not primarily designed to promote human rights, civil-military relations or sustainable peace. National interests will continue to influence regional intervention patterns.

Second, these precedents helped develop a collective African acceptance of African-led intervention as a response to intra-state wars. Partly because of this experience of ECOWAS engagement, AU member states approved the first armed peace operation, AMIB, in February 2003. This force, too, was severely hampered by its lack of material capabilities and financial resources. Funds coming mainly from the US, UK and EU were slowly disbursed and inadequate. Ultimately, South Africa provided most of the soldiers and equipment and absorbed most of the costs, and although the AU is under an obligation to reimburse South Africa for these costs, this is unlikely to happen (de Coning 2010a:20). Nonetheless, and as with the ECOWAS examples, AMIB displayed the AU's preparedness to shoulder responsibility for the management and resolution of conflicts on the continent. Today, 'African solutions to African problems' is a much cited vision or slogan associated with African conflict management.

Third, it is important to acknowledge that then, just as now, political realities brought about these first experiments in joint deployment. They were not the fruits of careful anticipation or strategy. In the immediate post-Cold War context, the UN's peace and security engagement in Africa evolved dramatically in step with the fast changing environment. The UNSC members 'disengaged' from the African continent and most civil wars after the early 1990s experiences in Somalia and Rwanda.[3] Unless clear strategic or economic interests were involved, UNSC members did not support a direct UN role in African civil wars. This made it evident that the UN could neither mobilise nor manage the enormous capabilities required for peace operations in many complex operational environments simultaneously. Thus, 'demand' in Africa will need to be met in cooperation with African actors.

Past examples of African-led regional and sub-regional peace operations have led some to caution that these these regional missions often step in as first-responders, using sometimes high levels of force, before they are transformed into complex UN peacebuilding operations (de Coning 2007:9). For instance, the coercive ECOMOG forces first stabilised the situation and collaborated with small UN observer missions, and these observer missions were transformed into comprehensive multidimensional UN peace operations: UNMIL (2003-still ongoing) and UNAMSIL (1999-2005). The result is that

---

3   There is a large literature on the nature and the changing conditions of UN peacekeeping in Africa. See for instance, Adebajo, Adekeye and Chris Landsberg, 'Back to the future: UN peacekeeping in Africa.' *International Peacekeeping*, Vol. 7, No 4 (2000): 161–88; Berman, Eric G. and Katie E. Sams, *Peacekeeping in Africa: Capabilities and Culpabilities*, Geneva: UNIDIR, 2000; Boulden, Jane (ed.), *Dealing With Conflict in Africa: The United Nations and Regional Organisations*, New York: Palgrave Macmillan, 2003; Carey, Margaret, 'Peacekeeping in Africa: Recent Evolution and Prospects', in Oliver Furley and Roy May (eds), *Peacekeeping in Africa*, 13–27, Aldershot: Ashgate, 1998; Clapham, Christopher. 'The United Nations and Peacekeeping in Africa', ISS Monograph no. 36 (1999); de Coning, Cedric, 'The Evolution of Peace Operations in Africa: Trajectories and Trends', *Journal of International Peacekeeping* 14, nos 1–2 (February 2010a): 6-26; Hentz, James, Frederik Söderbaum and Rodrigo Tavares, 'Regional Organisations and African Security: Moving the Debate Forward', *African Security* 2, nos. 2/3 (2009): 206–17; Murithi, Timothy, 'The African Union's Evolving Role in Peace Operations', African Security Review 17, no. 1 (2008): 70-82.

the highest risks and costs of peace operations are left to actors with the fewest resources to manage them. It has been argued that the result has been an 'apartheid-style' division of labour between developed and developing states, characterised by the unequal treatment of crises in Africa and the Middle East in terms of resources and political commitment (de Coning 2007:23; Bellamy and Williams 2007:195).

Why are 'jointness', support models or hybridity seen as a way forward?

Today, support for African peace operations and the AU-UN strategic peace and security partnership is a priority for the UN (Gelot 2012). There is growing recognition within UN circles that for the UN to achieve its own mandate, it needs to support the AU and other African organisations, because the UN cannot manage the conflicts in Africa on its own. This trend is not unique to Africa, but represents a more general shift towards burden-sharing between the UN and regional organisations (Gowan and Sherman 2012; Graham and Felicio 2006). Numerous senior UN officials and others, such as AU-UN high-level panel chief and former EU Commission President Romano Prodi, have stressed that if the UNSC wants to rely on Africa to do its own peacekeeping, it must empower the AU to do so (UNGA-UNSC 2008; Prodi 2009).

This shift is due to a number of complex factors. Africa is today seen as a strategically important continent by many major powers, yet when it comes to military involvement in African wars these same powers are seldom interested in committing troops or sufficient funds when the UN Secretariat calls for these. The UN's capacity or supply crisis has led many to criticise the organisation, especially the UNSC, for doing too little to ensure international peace and security, especially in Africa.

By April 2012, Africa accounted for seven of the UN's 16 peacekeeping missions. However, these seven included almost all of the UN's large multidimensional deployments. The combined strength of UN missions in Africa was 86,800 troops, close to 90 per cent of the worldwide total. Also included in the seven UN peacekeeping missions in Africa are 9,857 police officers and just over 12,500 international and local civilian personnel (DPKO 2012). The UNSC spends an estimated 60 per cent of its time discussing conflicts and concerns relating to Africa. As early as 1998, then UN Secretary-General Kofi Annan made clear the necessity of relying on regional and sub-regional initiatives in Africa, since the UN lacked the capacity, resources and expertise to address these conflicts on its own (Annan 1998).

These developments are not driven just by the UN's need to find local partners. By the early 1990s, African regional and sub-regional organisations such as the OAU, ECOWAS and SADC were showing increased willingness to rapidly authorise, man and lead very challenging peace operations on the continent (de Coning and Kasumba 2010:55). The Rwanda genocide, and UNSC unwillingness to respond to the crisis in timely fashion, stiffened the resolve of the OAU, and its successor, the AU, to develop its own capacity to deal with such crises in future. However, the AU and the sub-regional organisations face serious financial and material challenges and need external resources to sustain their peace operations (de Coning 2010a:22).

International endorsement and support is important for the effectiveness and success of peace operations (whether joint or not) and for the credibility of the UN peacekeeping enterprise. This is recognised in the DPKO/DFS 'New Horizon' policy initiative, which calls for a renewed global 'peacekeeping partnership' among the UNSC, contributing member states, host countries and the UN Secretariat. The partnership – the various actors having a shared understanding of the objectives of peace operations and a stake in their outcomes – is what UN peace operations depend on for their 'legitimacy, sustainability and global reach' (UN DPKO 2009:6–7). Similarly, former UN Secretary-General Kofi Annan's 1998 report on conflicts in Africa argued that the UN's legitimacy greatly depends upon African leaders and UN member states finding ways to act on their commitments to human security, including in Africa (Annan 1998).

Recently, policymakers have focused on how lesson-learning, information-sharing and technical assistance will make the AU-UN relationship work better. At play behind these policy discussions are, of course, the larger issues of authority, responsibility and efficiency. The UNSC guards its political authority. It has historically preferred a 'flexible approach' to regional-global delegation. UNSC members have not consistently applied the UN Charter's legal principles and are fearful of setting precedents. They thus prefer using inconsistent and ambiguous language on matters such as UNSC delegation and authorisation. Moreover, the UNSC has assumed a detached and pragmatic response to situations where regional actors and coalitions have acted without prior authorisation from it. Thus, the UNSC has permitted, through the insufficient establishment of oversight mechanisms, others to take the lead in peacekeeping and peace-enforcement operations without ensuring that those were informed by 'pro-UN Charter' motivations (Berman 1998:7).

Flexibility and 'constructive ambiguity' serve many useful purposes. They enable the UNSC to rapidly share the burdens with an array of actors while evading responsibility or future inconsistency if such efforts lead to anti-UN Charter or disappointing results. Some strong states and some regional actors have also at times preferred flexibility, so that they do not have to share authority over or ownership of a particular intervention with the UNSC. The Libya intervention has further stimulated debate on how UN-authorised missions, carried out by 'coalitions of the willing' or regional organisations, might be 'corralled' within the UN Charter's constitutional parameters.

Regional organisations, including the AU, have traditionally held that they have a comparative advantage over the UN at the early stage of responses to conflict. The assumption is that regional actors tend to be faster moving, with the contacts necessary to initiate peace talks without delay, and with troops standing by for fast deployment. The AU especially seems willing to engage in peace processes that entail high levels of risk, and require increasing robustness, in the belief that fragile peace processes need to be nurtured and that the international community cannot stand by until some form of ceasefire or peace agreement has been reached. Regional organisations can also help increase the political legitimacy of external interventions, especially since external interventions often stir up controversy in the host society for reasons of sovereignty, history or perceptions of lack of impartiality (de Coning and Kasumba 2010:61).

The AU has also shown itself keen to expand its autonomy of action. When the UNSC does not authorise UN troops in cases of mass atrocity, one argument is that regional actors might ensure rapid and more context-sensitive intervention. Despite outstanding legal issues and material weaknesses, populations at risk might prefer a small and underfunded response rather than none at all. Some regional actors might also ensure effective interventions, rapidly stabilising a very volatile situation. African states and institutions often cite situations where the AU should have been able to intervene, such as Angola, Somalia and, most dramatically, Rwanda. A peace and security structure in Africa was needed for those situations where the UN is unable or unwilling to authorise an intervention in a Rwanda-like case. The African Standby Force was structured with the Rwanda-scenario in mind: to act when the UN hesitates and to bridge the gap between the UNSC's adoption of a peace-operation mandate and the arrival of the mandated forces on the ground (de Coning and Kasumba 2010:74).

The AU took over from the OAU in 2002. It has been lauded as the first international organisation to have enshrined a right to forcibly intervene in one of its member states on humanitarian grounds, what Article 4(h) of the AU Charter refers to as grave circumstances: war crimes, genocide and crimes against humanity. Furthermore, AUPSC Protocol Article 16.1 states that the AU has 'the primary responsibility for promoting peace, security and stability in Africa', although Article 17.1 acknowledges that the UNSC 'has the primary responsibility for the maintenance of international peace and security'. Due to the AU's reliance on external funding, the AU membership's ability to take decisions independently on some strategic, operational and tactical aspects of its peace operations has been severely constrained to date (de Coning 2007:12). The regular AU budget relies heavily on contributions from its five largest member countries: Algeria, Egypt, Libya, Nigeria and South Africa. The AU Peace Fund has not attracted sizeable voluntary contributions from a great number of AU members. After the events of the Arab Spring, the AU faces a new funding reality, since Egypt and Libya may no longer be able or willing to contribute at their prior levels.

At the most recent AU summit in January 2012, during which the AU received its new headquarters complex as a gift from China, the significance of the partnership with non-African strategic partners such as China and the EU to the AU's ability to undertake peacemaking and peace operations on the continent was acknowledged. Emerging powers such as China, India, Brazil and Turkey are becoming important partners of the AU, but they have not yet made significant contributions in the area of peace and security. In these fields, the EU, the US and other Western donors remain the AU's most important strategic partners.

The unwillingness of some AU member states to contribute to the AU Peace Fund or to contribute troops to AU peace operations may suggest that African states do not see how these contributions further their national interests. The troops for AU peace operations mainly come from a small number of African states: South Africa provided most of the troops for the missions in Burundi and the Comoros; until early 2008, Uganda provided almost all the troops for the operation in Somalia; and Nigeria, Rwanda, Senegal and South Africa were the main troop-contributors for the AU's operation in Darfur (Williams 2009:619). Some African states do contribute troops to UN peacekeeping operations, but not to AU operations, while others tend to use their financial and military means only when their direct national interests are at stake. These decisions are probably informed by financial and resource constraints, but African regional actors need to clarify the political principles that should inform the relationship between member states, the AU and sub-regional organisations when it comes to contributing personnel and resources to Africa's peacemaking and peace support capacity. As the ASF develops, capacity to conduct independent peace operations might grow over time.

To date, ECOWAS, ECCAS, the Eastern African Standby Arrangement and SADC have the most developed capacity for use as part of future AU peace operations.

AU-UN Partnership in Support of African Peace Operations

The various issues outlined so far on the need for and difficulty of implementing joint support models have been the subject of much debate in practitioner and policy circles. The seminar convened by NAI, DHF and NUPI on 15 and 16 December 2011 was no exception, and the AU, EU and UN officials present paid particular attention to issues of funding, institutional capacity and political principles.

The seminar identified one of the key attributes of the AU-UN relationship as the increased political legitimacy the UN has derived in places like Darfur and Somalia through its partnership with the AU. Recent developments in the AU-UN peace and security partnership include the annual UNSC debates on peace and security in Africa, and the institution of an annual consultative meeting between the UNSC and AUPSC .

Another step towards a more visible and formalised relationship was taken on 1 July 2010, when the UN Office to the AU was established. This office is headed by an official at assistant secretary-general level, currently Zachary Muburi-Muita. It integrated the various UN peace and security presences in Addis Ababa: the UN liaison office; the UN's AU peace and support team; the UN planning team for AMISOM; and the administrative functions of the joint support and coordination mechanism of the AU-UN hybrid operation in Darfur.

Moreover, an AU-UN joint task force on peace and security was launched on 25 September 2010. The task force will work in coordination with the UNOAU and the AU's permanent observer mission to the UN and it will hold senior-level biannual meetings aimed at reviewing immediate and long-term strategic issues so as to enhance conflict prevention, peacekeeping and peacebuilding. The UN Secretariat is developing a strategic vision for UN-AU cooperation that involves closer interaction with the AU Commission to assist the UNSC and AUPSC in formulating cohesive positions and strategies. However, the UNSC permanent members want to avoid 'rigid' organisational structures between the UNSC and the AUPSC and are cautious about clearly defining the respective roles of the AU and UN in ensuring African stability.

The AU has called for a deepening of the strategic partnership between the two bodies based on what it refers to as the 'spirit' of Chapter VIII of the UN

Charter. It wants the UNSC to give 'due consideration' to the decisions of the AUPSC (AU 2012:45), even if the UNSC, given its primacy in the maintenance of international peace and security, cannot be expected to be bound by AUPSC decisions on matters pertaining to Africa. For the AU, 'ownership' and priority setting is a key principle, in part because this would help improve context-sensitivity in the agreed response (AU 2012:94).

The challenge, as the AU sees it, is how the AU and UN can apply the spirit of Chapter VIII without prejudicing the role of the UNSC, on one hand, and, on the other, without undermining or curtailing the AU's efforts to develop its own capacity to mount adequate responses to security challenges in Africa (AU 2012:88). The strategy needs to set out appropriate consultative decision-making frameworks, a clear division of labour and burden-sharing. The AU calls for an enhanced relationship between the UNSC's president and the AUPSC chair, and for an increased General Assembly role in determining the course of the partnership. The African position on financial support is that UN should provide funding for UNSC-authorised AU missions, citing the UN's primary responsibility for ensuring global peace and security and the consequent need to collaborate in a substantial way with regional peacekeeping.

The P5 remain reluctant to establish any generic or thematic decision on using the UN peacekeeping budget in this way. They prefer a case-by-case approach, such as was used for Darfur and Somalia. A UNSC resolution of January 2012 made the point that regional organisations have 'the responsibility to secure human, financial, logistical and other resources for their organisations, including through contributions by their members and support from partners' (UNSC 2012:Res 2033). The UNSC reaffirms its primacy, while recognising that the AU is 'well positioned' to understand the causes of armed conflict in Africa and that this is useful in trying to prevent or resolve these conflicts (UNSC 2012:Res 2033). In this way, the resolution carefully refutes any sense of equivalence between the UNSC and AUPSC. The resolution requested the UN Secretary-General, in consultation with the AU, to 'conduct a comprehensive analysis of lessons learned' from UNAMID and AMISOM. It decided:

> ... in consultation with the African Union Peace and Security Council to elaborate further ways of strengthening relations between the two Councils including through achieving more effective annual consultative meetings, the holding of timely consultations, and collaborative field missions of the two Councils, as appropriate, to formulate cohesive positions and strategies on a case by case basis in dealing with conflict situations in Africa. (UNSC 2012:Res 2033)

Participants at the December 2011 seminar raised the point that from the AU perspective, partnership with the UN is expected to move the discussion towards greater funding predictability and sustainability. In theory, the AU Commission should benefit from the vast experience of UN staff in managing peace operations, but, in practice, many of the UN 'experts' providing advice to the AU have limited peacekeeping experience. As many of these experts are from Africa, they might as well be hired directly by the AU. The problem is thus not that Africa lacks peacekeeping experience, but that the AU seems to lack the ability to mobilise that experience, probably due to weak institutional capacity within the AU and sub-regional organisations.

If that diagnose is correct, UN expertise, however professional, would be rendered equally ineffective by the AU's inability to absorb and act on the advice offered. Working together more closely will, it is hoped, lead to increased knowledge transfer and institutional development. Anyidoho's paper in this volume makes the point that working jointly in a conflict zone will help senior officials, troops and police officers deal more effectively with conflicts in different areas in Africa. Since the AU is not financially and logistically independent enough to sustain its peace operations on it its own, joint missions will, it is hoped, help bridge this capacity gap. Proximity to the UN and support is important in the 'transition period' as the AU reaches its full potential. UN support of African missions will help draw international attention to and keep it focused on African conflicts. The AU-UN partnership is also a symbolic way of recognising that wars in Africa are not purely African problems but global security issues worthy of attention.

Seminar participants discussed several factors that to date have jeopardised synergies in the relationship. On the AU side, participants focused on the organisation's role, budget issues and political principles. As to the UN, participants stressed the organisation's need for P5 support and the pros and cons of the existing peace operations culture .

The AU's strategic and planning capacity for peace operations is an aspect of the AU's role in peace and security. The AU Commission and AU member states need to formulate what the AU's role is in peace and security on the continent. What are the comparative advantages of the AU and can one leverage them? Achieving an agreed vision could increase AU member states' buy in for or ownership of the development of the African peace and security structure. It would help prevent duplication of effort by the UN, RECs and other peace and security actors. From this strategic debate would then emerge ideas on how best to improve strategic guidance and direction, strategy and military planning in the AUPSC-AU Peace Support Operations Division relationship.

Problem with the African Solutions for African Problems Model

The contributions from African member states to the AU Peace Fund have been disappointing. The seminar discussed the possible significance of this pattern. Could it be that many AU member states do not support the AU's direction in developing its peace and security architecture, and hence withhold funding? If so, the AU is unlikely to develop into a strong organisation or a credible voice on African peace and security issues. Could it be that AU member states feel the AU's peace and security agenda is a donor-driven project, or is developing into a more supranational structure than they support? Or do the majority of AU member states support the current process, but are simply unable to contribute financially? Or could it be that more AU member states could contribute financially, but are comfortable with donors filling this gap? It is high time to pause and reflect on these questions, and to ensure there is no gap between member state expectations on one hand, and AU Commission policies and projects on the other.

Participants suggested that AU member states start treating AU peace operations as the flagship enterprise it has been presented as to the world. One question raised by several participants was: If AU member states do not invest long-term in the AU's peace and security role, how can the organisation ask donors to continue funding the AU's peace and security architecture? The question has gained in importance against the background of the Arab Spring. And with recession facing many large economies, donors are likely to increase demands for accountability and transparency. They are more likely to fund viable projects, that is, an AU peace and security structure supported and funded by African states also.

Another area of concern for seminar participants was the underdeveloped political principles underpinning the AU peace and security structure. The AU does not have a clear position on non-compliance by member states with AU rules and communiqués. Here again we see the tension between the AU's inter-state and supranational nature. Some AU member states treat the AU as simply an inter-state forum. States hosting AU peace operations attempt to direct the pace of the missions or use them as tools, with varying responses. A few participants observed that host state withdrawal/manipulation of consent is a political, not a technical or operational, issue, and that the AU needs a position on this rather than a reactive/selective approach. There was also a sense that tensions in the relations among AU, RECs and the UN jeopardise the smooth functioning of support models. It is not always clear to the UN or other donors when they should approach the AU or a REC on a specific issue.

The UN Secretariat has a well-established culture and bureaucracy of how to initiate, plan and manage a peace operation. Reform of or change in the bureaucracy takes a very long time. The seminar noted that the large and rigid bureaucracy and earlier development of procedures and standards to improve the well-being and performance of UN peacekeepers in the field (DPKO peace operations) may not meet the realities and core needs of African peace operations today. The UN sometimes has to go beyond its own guidelines to help the AU respond to day-to-day operational needs. This can put UN Secretariat officials as well as state representatives in an uncomfortable position as they try to avoid precedents for the future. In turn, this type of organisational conflict may undermine AU-UN collaboration in peace operations.

The seminar also touched on the importance of a partnership resting on a sense of mutual benefit and complementarity, with each organisation valuing the complementary role of the other, and the respective strengths. To date, officials in Addis Ababa have occasionally felt bypassed in peace and security decisions. The UN Secretariat and influential UNSC members sometimes see the benefit of bringing the AU fully on board, but sometimes act as if they already have all the expertise, capacity and legitimacy to deal with a certain situation. On the AU side, there is a wish for the relationship to be more reciprocal, and for the AUPSC to be consistently consulted on issues of African peace and security.

The above overview underscores the need for broad debate on support models. We cannot limit discussion to how to find willing funders, the AU's financial limitations and the world economic situation. We also cannot look at isolated examples, such as the specifics of AU-UN collaboration in Sudan's conflicts. For this reason, the seminar aimed at ranging beyond traditional critiques of specific peace operations and took a more holistic approach to and reflective stance on support models in general.

2. Exploring the Benefits and Disadvantages of Hybrid and Other Support Models for Peace Operations in Africa

Kwesi Aning and Mustapha Abdallah

Introduction

This paper explores the ongoing debate on hybrid and support models for peacekeeping in Africa, focusing on the benefits and disadvantages of the hybrid mission in Darfur, UNAMID. The paper argues that, while peacekeeping operations have resulted in relative peace in countries such as Liberia, Sierra Leone and Burundi, leading to democratic development, other conflicts such as in Somalia, DRC and Sudan have continued with varying degrees of intensity despite the presence of peacekeepers. They often make headlines as some of the most endemic and complex conflicts in Africa. UNAMID, the first UN hybrid mission was adopted in response to the complex nature of the Sudan conflict and particularly to the failure of its predecessor, the AU Mission in Sudan to accomplish its objectives, namely, to halt the large-scale killings and displacement of the civilian population in Darfur (Holt and Berkman 2006).

Four years after the adoption of Resolution 1769 to commence UNAMID operations, questions have been raised about the operation's efficacy. Thus, many commentators are unsatisfied with its contribution to the protection of civilians and in addressing general security challenges. From the existing literature and the ongoing debate, the UN is not likely to propose this approach again in future peace operations. However, the AU appears to support hybrid missions as an alternative model for peacekeeping in Africa.

In this paper, we examine the benefits and disadvantages/challenges of the UNAMID hybrid mission and suggest possible collaborative options to improve existing frameworks. It must be noted that UNAMID was the first experiment in hybrid missions in the UN's history of peacekeeping. As a result, and especially given the size and complex nature of the Sudan conflict, challenges were bound to emerge. However, we argue that this does not justify the discontinuation of hybrid missions. There is, therefore, a need to explore options that could, after further study, allow for the eventual adoption of an alternative model, given the multiple challenges and complexity of emerging conflicts in Africa.

ECOMOG Model in Liberia: cooperation and conflict between ECOWAS and UN

In 1989, an attack was launched into Liberia by Charles Taylor and the National Patriotic Front of Liberia (NPFL) aimed at removing Samuel Kanyon Doe (Aboagye 1999). In August 1990, following peace moves initiated by the ECOWAS regional organisation and the initial refusal of the UN and the US to intervene, ECOWAS mandated a monitoring group, ECOMOG, to intercede, citing humanitarian reasons that had the potential to undermine regional stability (Hutchful 1999). It was also mandated to supervise a cease-fire and to establish an interim government, which was to organise an election to be held after a year (ECOWAS 1990).

Although ECOMOG was hailed as a landmark in regional peacekeeping in Africa, it was replaced by the UN observer mission (UNOMIL) in 1994, after several peace talks in Bamako, Lomé, Yamoussoukro and Monrovia had failed. The only successful talks were brokered in Cotonou, Benin (Cotonou Agreement) in 1993 under the auspices of the UN, ECOWAS and the OAU. According to Monie Captan, ECOMOG as a peacekeeping force had serious issues in engendering confidence among the warring factions (interview Monie Captan, 2011). Consequently, the involvement of UNOMIL was perceived as strategic and this entity was expected to support ECOMOG in ensuring compliance with and impartial implementation of the agreement by all parties. It also took the pressure off ECOWAS, a sub-regional body that was not originally established to undertake peacekeeping operations. ECO-MOG's replacement by UNOMIL culminated in a UN presence in Liberia with the mandate as well as financial and military might to ensure that lasting peace returned to Liberia (interview Monie Captan, 2011). Its presence was, therefore, significant and marked the first instance in the history of the UN of cooperation with a sub-regional peacekeeping mission in peace operations.

Despite the lack of progress in the implementation of the Cotonou Agreement, the cooperation between UNOMIL and ECOWAS resulted in the successful conduct of elections in 1997 and led to the investiture of Charles Taylor as president. Upon expiration of its mandate, UNOMIL was replaced by the UN Peacebuilding Support Office in Liberia (UNOL) in 1997, which was tasked with assisting the new government to consolidate the peace following the elections.

The relative peace and stability that followed the 1997 elections was short-lived as governance challenges drove deep wedges between the government and opposition party leaders, reigniting the conflict in 2003. This resulted in the establishment of the UN Mission in Liberia (UNMIL) primarily to facilitate the efficient implementation of the 2003 comprehensive peace agreement signed in Accra (UNSC Resolution 1503). Soon after UNMIL took over peacekeeping responsibilities from the ECOWAS mission in Liberia (ECOMIL), security in the capital improved dramatically and the political process progressed. In addition, the use of relatively new mechanisms such as strategic deployment stocks, the rapid deployment team roster and the pre-mandate commitment authority helped expedite deployment (UN Peacekeeping Best Practices Unit 2004).

Worthy of note is that the deployment of UNMIL, like that of UNOMIL, was contingent on the initial stabilisation interventions by ECOMOG and ECOMIL. Even more important is the coordination of efforts by UNOMIL and UNMIL under the command and control of the UN. In the case of Liberia, it seemed that cooperation between the UN and the regional bodies was the *sine qua non* for successful peacekeeping operations in Africa.

UN-AU Collaboration

Article 52(1) of the UN Charter provides that:

> Nothing in the present Charter precludes the existence of regional arrangements or agencies for dealing with such matters relating to the maintenance of international peace and security as are appropriate for regional action, provided that such arrangements or agencies and their activities are consistent with the Purposes and Principles of the United Nations. (UN doc. 1945)

For its part, Article 17(1) of the protocol relating to the establishment of the AUPSC cites Chapter VIII of the UN Charter as the basis for its relationship with the UN and, most importantly, acknowledges the primacy of the UNSC in maintaining international peace and security. The protocol directs the AUPSC to cooperate with the UNSC, '… which has the primary responsibility for the maintenance of international peace and security' (AU 2002, Art. 17.1).

On the basis of these provisions, both the UN and the AU recognise the importance of fostering cooperation and collaboration. Consequently, in November 2006 Kofi Annan, then-UN Secretary-General and Alpha Oumar Konaré, then-AU chairperson, signed a declaration on Enhancing UN-AU

Cooperation: Framework for the Ten Year Capacity Building Programme for the AU. The declaration set out to increase cooperation between the two organisations and to enhance UN system-wide engagement with the AU, its regional and sub-regional organisations and the New Partnership for Africa's Development (NEPAD) to meet the challenges of the African continent, including issues of peacekeeping and peacebuilding (AU 2012). Similarly, in 2008, the UN Secretary-General, Ban Ki Moon called on the UNSC to properly define the role of regional organisations and to ensure that a structured system of cooperation is put in place to ensure coherence of international and regional responses to existing and emerging conflicts.

These calls have resulted in efforts to deepen cooperation and collaboration between the UN and AU. The establishment of the UNOAU in July 2010, headed by an assistant secretary-general, is, therefore, a welcome attempt to integrate the mandates of the different UN offices to the AU, namely the UN Liaison Office to the AU (UNLO-AU), the AU peacekeeping support team and the UN planning team for AMISOM and the joint support coordination mechanism for UNAMID. Moreover, the inauguration of the AU-UN joint task force on peace and security in September 2010 further strengthened the partnership between UN Secretariat and AU Commission, and it now also serves as a forum in which senior management of the two institutions can exchange views on matters of common concern and agree on common actions, including peacekeeping. Despite the legal and institutional arrangements for cooperation, the experience of missions, particularly UNAMID, discussed below shows that more needs to be done to ensure cooperative arrangements for peacekeeping are practically effective.

Advantages of the Hybrid Mission

In examining the benefits of hybrid missions, it is important to understand the reasons for the failure of AMIS. This happened partly because the AU lacks the logistical, personnel and financial capacity necessary for peacekeeping in Darfur. However, the AU has demonstrated willingness and capacity to respond to emergencies to prevent mass abuse of the human rights of civilian populations. Through UNAMID, therefore, cooperation between the AU and UN in Darfur provided an opportunity for both organisations to exploit their comparative advantages, with the AU harnessing troops, responding as a stabilisation force, reducing civilian casualties and maintaining relative peace and security with funds and logistics provided by the UN component.

A comparative analysis of the missions to Burundi and Sudan, on the one hand, and to Somalia, on the other, shows the extent to which cooperative or hybrid peacekeeping missions could speed up the processes of ensuring peace. In Burundi, even though AMIB did establish relative peace in most provinces, its replacement by the UN Peace Operation in Burundi and the latter's subsequent transformation into the UN Integrated Office in Burundi (BINUB) in December 2006 contributed to lasting peace. By October 2006, some 20,000 militia and military personnel had been demobilised with the involvement of the UN (Nhlapo 2006). In effect, the UN bailed out the AU from what could have been a drawn out intervention. On the other hand, AMIS could not execute its mandate efficiently because it remained largely an AU force lacking in the necessary operational resources.

Cooperation between the UN and the AU is also beneficial in instances where the UN is not interested in intervening. Since the withdrawal of the UN Operation in Somalia (UNOSOM) and the US-led Unified Task Force (UNITAF) in 1993 following several military disasters and a lack of progress in peace talks, AMISOM has solely borne the burden of peacekeeping in Somalia. In a 13 April 2007 report, UN Secretary-General Ban Ki Moon indicated that Somalia was too dangerous for a peacekeeping operation as there was no peace to keep and there was no way the UN could replace AMISOM. However, because of existing cooperation between the two organisations and the fact that the UN has the primary responsibility to maintain international peace and security, it supports AMISOM through the UN trust fund. In 2007, for example, the UN approved a limited logistical support package of US$71 million in contributions for AMISOM. The EU has also supported AMISOM with €15.5 million through the African Peace Support Facility (EU Council 2010).

Another benefit hybrid missions offer is the large number of peacekeepers from TCCs outside Africa. Many African states and individuals are reluctant to accept postings under AU-sponsored missions because, unlike the UN, the AU lacks the financial capacity to meet its commitments and to supply the logistics and equipment necessary to ensure the safety and security of peacekeepers, especially in complex environments such as Somalia and Sudan. When AMIS was established in 2004, it was a small operation of 60 military observers, supported by a protection force of 300. By the end of 2006, AMIS had just 7,000 uniformed personnel. This was inadequate, given the fragile security situation on the ground. In contrast, UNAMID was to receive troops from outside Africa if African nations were unable to meet force requirements. Though the Sudanese government has consistently resisted inclusion of non-African troops in UNAMID, by September 2011, 39 countries had pledged troops and 35 had pledged police personnel. Of the 39 countries that pledged troops, 17 are outside Africa, as are 16 of the police contributing countries.[4] This approach is aimed at augmenting the limited number of troops provided by African countries to AMIS. The net effect was an increased presence of peacekeepers to deliver on the mandate of protecting civilians and to address general security challenges.

Challenges of the UNAMID Hybrid Mission

This section first addresses the challenges specific to the complex Sudanese geographical and political environment and general challenges associated with peace operations.

Geography

An understanding of the geographical location of Sudan is critical to appreciating the complexity and enduring nature of the conflict. Until recently, when South Sudan was carved out as an independent state, Sudan was the largest country in Africa and shared borders with nine countries, namely Eritrea and Ethiopia to the east; Kenya, Uganda and DRC to the south; the Central African Republic, Chad and Libya to the west; and Egypt to the north. Of these, however, Chad, Eritrea, Libya and Egypt have been the most prominent in terms of interference in the conflict in Darfur or of the cross-border implications of and interference in the internal conflict (ICG 2007:2). This proximity and the broader international dimension of conflict (Annan 1997) and the varied interests of the countries in supporting one rebel group or the other, has undermined UNAMID's efforts to execute its mandate (Aning 1997). Particularly as a result of economic backwardness and weak state institutions, enclaves have been created for rebel groups in neighbouring border states such as Chad and the Central African Republic, from which rebel groups launch attacks against their home governments. Besides this, there are the interests of neighbouring governments in ousting each other, for example Chad's backing of the forces in Darfur and the attempt by the Khartoum government to topple the regime in N'Djamena. This has been exacerbated particularly by

---

4   Military personnel: Bangladesh, Canada, China, Ecuador, Germany, Guatemala, Indonesia, Italy, Jordan, Malaysia, Mongolia, Nepal, Netherlands, Pakistan, Republic of Korea, Thailand, Yemen. Police personnel: Bangladesh, Canada, Fiji, Germany, Indonesia, Jamaica, Jordan, Kyrgyzstan, Malaysia, Nepal, Norway, Pakistan, Palau, Philippines, Tajikistan, Turkey and Yemen (UNDPKO 2011).

Darfur's geographic isolation, harsh climate, limited food and water supplies and poor infrastructure to support UNAMID's mission.

Political

Achieving the broad mandate of UNAMID was dependent on cooperation and compliance by the Sudanese government and other parties to the peace process. However, even prior to the passage of Resolution 1769 establishing UNAMID, Al-Bashir had opposed the transition from AMIS to a UN Mission in Sudan. Although UNMIS was subsequently approved by Resolution 1706, it lacked international support and faced obstruction by the Sudanese government.

Similarly, the Sudanese government strongly opposed the deployment of UNAMID at every step. The Sudanese military attacked a UNAMID convoy less than two weeks after its inauguration and has continually obstructed deployment of the force by refusing to approve the list of TCCs provided by the UN and AU, imposing restrictions on UNAMID flights, delaying the release of UNAMID equipment from Port Sudan and failing to provide sufficient land for bases in Darfur.

Closely allied with Al-Bashir's opposition is the existence of multiple rebel groups, which have also hindered the smooth operation of UNAMID in Darfur. Rebel forces were reluctant to move towards a peace agreement and ceasefire. Some key rebel leaders have been unwilling to participate in the unified UN-AU peace process, to the detriment of the Darfuri people. The fight in the western region of Darfur involved rebel forces, including the Sudan Liberation Movement/Army and the Justice and Equality Movement, among more than a dozen others. A Human Rights Watch report indicates that there is close coordination between the Janjaweed militias and Rally for Democracy and Liberty rebels, and there is circumstantial evidence that not just the Janjaweed but also the RDL receive material and other support from Sudanese government forces to perpetrate violence (HRW 2006).

Economic/Financial

One critical element determining the success of peacekeeping missions is adequate financial resources. This is important for the effective operations of missions in terms of deployment of troops and the provision of logistics and equipment. Prior to the establishment of UNAMID, AMIS had depended largely on external partners to finance the mission and to provide technical advice and support (International Peace Academy 2007). In the face of dwindling global resources and the rising cost of peacekeeping (about $7.8 billion a year) (UNDPKO 2009), UNAMID, like AMIS, has faced and continues to face similar financial challenges. The hybrid operation was expected to cost more than $2.5 billion in its first year, including the start-up cost. The initial understanding was that Africa and most Third World countries would provide manpower, while the West would provide the necessary logistical support. Due to economic and financial challenges, neither the AU nor the UN could provide the manpower and logistics for the UNAMID force. The available manpower in 2008 was just over 9,000 of the expected 26,000. The troops already in place, including the old AU force and two new battalions, lacked essential equipment, such as sufficient armoured personnel carriers and helicopters to carry out even the most rudimentary of peacekeeping tasks. Onoja states that the troops were so poorly provisioned that they had to buy their own paint to turn their green AU helmets into blue UN helmets (2008:42). In order to strengthen the capacity of UNAMID, a budget of US$1,689 billion has been approved for the operation of UNAMID from 1 July 2011 to 30 June 2012 (UNGA 2011). Despite this, donor fatigue will continue to pose a challenge for the operation.

Mandate

Although the initial mandate for UNAMID was comparatively comprehensive, two important provisions were lacking. The threat of sanctions against the Khartoum regime in the event of non-compliance and authorisation of UNAMID to seize or collect illegal arms in Darfur in terms of a UN-mandated Darfur arms embargo were both stripped from the final version of Resolution 1769. This was in spite of the fact that the drafters were well aware of the role of neighbouring states in fuelling the conflict, and the likelihood of infiltration by armed rebels who could exacerbate the conflict.

Recognising the inherent deficiencies of Resolution 1769 and determining that the situation in Sudan constituted a threat to international peace and security, the UNSC decided to extend the UNAMID mandate a further 12 months to 31 July 2012. Consequently, the UNSC adopted at its 6,597th meeting Resolution 2003 on 29 July 2011 (UNSC 2011). While the resolution mandates UNAMID to monitor for violations of existing arms embargos, it lacks provisions condemning the government of Sudan for its obstruction and harassment of humanitarian workers over the past four years (UNSC 2011).

Options for Future UN-AU Collaboration/Hybrid Missions

Despite the challenges above, there are options for the UN and AU to explore collaboratively in their pursuit of efficient and effective peace operations and maintaining global peace and security.

First, there is a need for enhanced cooperation between the UN and AU in addressing the security challenges on the continent. As stated earlier, although the UN in Article 52(1) of its Charter recognises the role of regional organisations, there is a lack of clarity in its interpretation. On the other hand, the AU also recognises the need to promote enhanced cooperation and partnership with the UN as provided for in Article 17(1) of the 2002 Protocol on Establishment of the Peace and Security Council. However, the UN has yet to develop an outline for cooperation. What is critical, therefore, for the UN and AU is revisiting the 2006 Declaration on Enhancing UN-AU Cooperation: Framework for the Ten Year Capacity Building Programme for the AU. This should be an important guide for more formalised cooperation to meet the challenges of the African continent.

In pursuit of this cooperative agenda, each organisation should exploit the unique advantages of the other. The AU, for instance, has demonstrated capacity to intervene in situations where arguably there is no peace to keep. In Burundi and Sudan, the AU intervened with AMIB and AMIS respectively to stabilise the situation. This, according to De Coning, is needed for long-term post-conflict resolution (de Coning 2010b). While the initial intervention by the AU is important to protect civilians, the UN over the years has also demonstrated a capacity, which the AU lacks, to sustain long-term missions. The replacement of AMIB by ONUB and its subsequent transformation into BINUB in December 2006 contributed to lasting peace to Burundi. Similarly, the transformation of AMIS into UNAMID was important in addressing the security challenges in Darfur.

Second, future mandates for hybrid missions must be comprehensive and reflect the size of the peacekeeping force and the broader security challenges in the mission state. Drafters should either have an in-depth knowledge of the political and security situation in the mission state or must include local experts to advise on possible loopholes that might undermine the effectiveness of the mandate. Moreover, issues of state consent should be re-examined. Although Resolution 1769 establishing UNAMID was unanimously adopted, it was deficient in some respects. For instance, as indicated earlier, the threat of sanctions against the Khartoum regime in the event of non-compliance and authorisation of UNAMID to seize or collect arms that were in Darfur in violation of the UN-mandated arms embargo were dropped from the final version of Resolution 1769, basically because of the issue of state consent. Similarly, Resolution 2003, which extended UNAMID from 29 July 2011 to June 2012, also failed to condemn the government of Sudan for obstructing and harassing humanitarian workers.

Third, the resource and capacity needs of the AU to undertake peace operations are critical. With few notable exceptions, most African states are too economically constrained to contribute to the Peace Fund and support peace operations in Africa. For instance, since January 2006, 75 per cent of the AU's regular budget has been paid for by only five countries: Algeria, Egypt, Libya, Nigeria and South Africa (each paying 15 per cent of the total) (AUEC 2011). Libya also assists several poorer African countries in meeting their commitments to the AU (Downie 2011). With the death of Gaddafi, it can be argued that support packages from Libya will decline significantly. There is, therefore, a need for hybrid missions that place the responsibility to provide finance and logistics on developed and Western states. Though there are several African states with considerable UN peacekeeping experience (Senegal, Kenya, Botswana, Nigeria, Ghana, Zimbabwe), the AU has marginal economic resources to support these states in conducting sustained and effective military operations. The peacekeepers have only been able to execute their duties through combat support resources and financial aid from Western countries and the UN. The reality has been that logistical and financial constraints preclude most African states from participating individually in peace operations except with sustainment, strategic lift and financing from an external source. According to the 2010 assessment study, part of the AU's challenge in peacekeeping can be attributed to the non-operationalisation of the various pillars of APSA, particularly the ASF. When operationlised, the ASF will enable the AU to respond to conflicts by deploying peacekeeping forces to undertake interventions pursuant to Articles 4(h) and (j) of the AU's Constitutive Act. The UN and bilateral donor agencies should, therefore, coordinate their efforts to develop a much stronger APSA and the operationalisation of its pillars, particularly the ASF, as a complement to their own peace operations.

Finally, the complexities of modern African conflicts require the collaboration of the UN, which has over 60 years of peacekeeping experience. Through this collaboration, the AU could learn from the strategies previously adopted by the UN to achieve peace.

Conclusion

What the paper has sought to discuss is the viability of hybrid missions as alternative models for peacekeeping in response to the complexities of modern African conflicts. It further assessed whether the adoption of UNAMID following the failure of AMIS was efficient and effective in achieving its core mandate of protecting civilians and, therefore, whether this format should be adopted by the UN in future peace operations. Clearly, the study has noted that the need for cooperation and collaboration in peacekeeping is not new in Africa. At the sub-regional level, it is traceable to the UN's establishment of UNOMIL and later UNMIL in Liberia to support and complement the efforts of ECOMOG and ECOMIL.

At the continental level, both the UN and AU have provisions in their respective charters and the constitutive acts for collaboration in ensuring peace and security. Consequently, since the inauguration of the AU in 2002, Kofi Annan and Ban Ki-Moon have taken steps to strengthen cooperation between the two organisations. In addition to contributing to the creation of the joint support coordination mechanism and joint task force, they helped to establish UNAMID.

However, as with AMIS, UNAMID has faced multiple challenges specific to the geopolitical context of Sudan but also illustrative of general peacekeeping challenges such as funding, logistics and equipment. Given that this was the first experiment in mounting a hybrid mission, such challenges were to be expected. What is worthy of emphasis is that given the complexities of modern conflicts and the rising cost of peacekeeping, it will be difficult if not impossible for the AU alone to undertake successful peacekeeping missions. The experiences of ECOMOG and ECOMIL in Liberia, AMIS in Sudan and AMISOM in Somalia demonstrate the lack of capacity by ECOWAS and the AU to singlehandedly ensure peace in conflict-ridden environments. The peace and security councils of ECOWAS, the AU and UNSC should, therefore, deepen their collaboration and explore further opportunities for hybrid missions in Africa. The relative success of UNAMID in bringing peace to Sudan should be an encouraging example of the potential of hybrid missions as an alternative model. The solution, therefore, lies in the collaborative efforts of the UN on one hand and regional and sub-regional organisations such as the AU and ECOWAS on the other.

3. Experiences of the African Mission in Sudan (AMIS) and the AU-UN Hybrid Mission in Sudan (UNAMID)

Henry Anyidoho

Introduction

Conflicts in Africa vary in nature from inter-state to intra-state. While precolonial history has recorded a number of revolutionary wars of independence, the Cold War, on the other hand, held together segments of ethnic, religious or tribal groupings under a 'state' structure. In sub-Saharan Africa in recent times the more dominant conflict has been the intra-state type, which has become more pronounced. Particularly after the end of the Cold War, different ethnic, religious or tribal groupings began to assert their influence and to assume a greater identity, as also to seek a fair share of national power and wealth.

Case of Darfur

Background documents available at the AUPSC in Addis Ababa indicate that the origins of the conflict in Darfur can be traced to the British colonial administration (which began in 1916) and beyond. Before the colonial era, Darfur was an independent sultanate with the Fur as the ruling group. Other tribes found in Darfur in this period included Masahit, Zaghawa, Berti, Tama, Gimir, Tunjur, Meidob, Daja, Birgid, Burg and others. The Fur, who were essentially farmers, occupied the slopes of the Jebel Mara mountains and surrounding areas. They expanded south and westwards, in the process absorbing other smaller ethnic groups, both Arab and non-Arab. A key issue in the conflict is land. British colonial administrators introduced the idea of tribal '*dars*' or homelands with defined territories and under community paramount chiefs, who had jurisdiction over land allocations.

This arrangement presented two problems. First, it was never formally recognised in subsequent Sudanese laws, and two, the nomadic groups in the central belt of Darfur were never granted their own '*dars*', owing to their way of life. With an expanding population and the attendant ecological degradation, nomadic groups were compelled to look for pasture outside their traditional grazing areas. At the same time, the farmers were expanding their land under cultivation and fencing off parcels to conserve pasture for their own animals. A conflict was bound to erupt and since the 1980s successive federal and state governments have been unable to put a halt to it. The southward and westward expansion of Arab camel herders destroyed farms and water sources for irrigation in an attempt to assert land ownership: this is one of the principal causes of the conflict.

The other principal cause is the neglect and marginalisation of the people of Darfur in national politics, which has been exploited by Islamist movements. Following a series of misunderstandings and the split of the movement from the government, the crisis took on regional/ethnic characteristics. Political realignments occurred, with Nile valley Arabs making opportunistic alliances with the Janjaweed militia north of Darfur. The other groups opposed these alliances, with the Justice and Equality Movement and the Sudanese Liberation Movement/Army emerging as a result. SLA/JEM insurgency against the regime in Khartoum began in 2003. The humanitarian crisis that resulted from the displacement, massacres and famine moved the world to act. Former UN Secretary-General Kofi Annan visited Darfur on 29 June 2004 followed by General Colin Powell, US Secretary of State, on 30 June 2004.

On 8 April 2004, the government of Sudan, SLM/A and JEM signed the humanitarian ceasefire agreement in N'Djamena, capital of Chad, under the auspices of the AU and with the government of Chad acting as mediator. This was followed by the signing of the agreements on and modalities for establishing a ceasefire commission and observers to Darfur in Addis Ababa on 28 May 2004. Articles 3 and 4 of the ceasefire agreement mandated the formation of a ceasefire commission tasked with monitoring and reporting to a joint implementation commission (JIC), Chadian mediators and the international community on compliance with the agreements by the parties. Between 7-13 May 2004, the AU had dispatched an assessment mission to Darfur, which had recommended the immediate establishment of a humanitarian ceasefire commission. This commission became operational on 9 June 2004. In the same month, the AU deployed 60 military observers along with a small protection force of 310, whose main task was to provide the military observers and members of the ceasefire commission with security in the conduct of their duties. No sooner had AMIS been deployed than the AU recognised how inadequate it was. The ability to provide direction and support to AMIS was stretched to the limit. The AU mission was revised and upgraded several times in terms of numbers and equipment, but it became obvious that it could not cope with the complexities of the situation. The AU on its own, in a communiqué issued on

12 January 2006 in Addis Ababa, expressed support in principle for a transition from AMIS to UN operations in Darfur. Several steps were subsequently taken resulting in the passing of UNSC Resolution 1706 on August 2006. However, the resolution was rejected by the government of Sudan and the UN and AU had to return to the drawing board. After high level consultations in Addis Ababa on 16 November 2006, a decision was taken to establish a three step approach to peacekeeping in Darfur, at the same time stressing the political process and the ceasefire agreement. The first step was a light support package to the AU mission followed by a heavy support package and finally a UN-AU hybrid operations in Darfur. Subsequently the UNSC passed Resolution 1769 on 31 July 2007 to establish the joint mission in Darfur. On 31 December 2007, the transfer of authority from AMIS to UNAMID took place in Darfur. Since then, UNAMID has been confronted with many problems.

From the beginning of peacekeeping operations in Darfur, the AU and UN have worked together, but the relationship has not always been very clear. The main reason for this is that the UN has been closely involved in AU efforts on Darfur since the signing of the N'Djamena humanitarian ceasefire agreement on 8 April 2004. All actions or steps taken by the AU equally involved the UN. The very first reconnaissance carried out soon after the N'Djamena agreement and the subsequent deployment of the AU's 60 military observers and 310 strong protection force involved the UN. The UN followed up by establishing the assistance cell in Addis Ababa to provide strategic guidance to the mission in Darfur. Every subsequent action, including repeated reviews of the size of AMIS, involved UN. The AU took the lead, and the UN encouraged its leadership or ownership role and was prepared to play what Jean-Marie Guéhenno, former under secretary-general in DPKO, described as a 'back-stopping' role in support of AU efforts. It was also clearly stated that hybrid operations should be under UN rules and regulations. The manner in which the hybrid mission has so far been administered must have informed the UN support package for the AU Mission in Somalia.

Deployment

The first major problem was the slow pace of deployment. Since Resolution 1769 clearly stated the mission had to be predominantly African, and because most African countries do not have ready-to-deploy troops, it took a very long time to have even infantry units on the ground in Darfur. The countries that pledged troops had to rely on Western donor countries for vehicles and other essential equipment in order to deploy. There were also difficulties with formed police units. While UNAMID inherited poorly equipped infantry contingents from AMIS, it had no formed police units at all at its disposal. One year after UNAMID came into existence, only one of the 19 police units provided for in the resolution to stabilise the large and volatile IDP camps had been deployed. Colleagues currently serving in Darfur are in a better position to inform us on the present situation.

Political Situation and International Criminal Court

As the deployment problems continued, there were other serious and complex issues that UNAMID had to contend with. First, the Darfur peace agreement was signed by only the government of Sudan and the Mini Minawe faction of the SLM and was not working in Darfur. Instead, the signing of the peace agreement resulted in the fragmentation of rebel movements. One of them, calling itself the Liberation and Justice Movement, was in Doha holding discussions with the mediation team at the time I left the mission.

Another significant event was that while attempts were under way to find a political settlement for the crisis, the International Criminal Court at the Hague indicted President Omar Al-Bashir for war crimes. At that time, July 2008, UNAMID had to relocate some of its staff temporarily while the operation was still deploying! The security level for of the mission was raised and there was real panic among staff. There was also the issue of whether UNAMID should do any business with the indicted president. For those at the helm of affairs in Darfur, we had no choice for prosecuting our mandate but to deal with the number one man in Sudan. I do not believe that the international community has yet recognised the strength of the Sudanese government. Sudan is perhaps the first country with a reasonably strong government that has had to accept two peacekeeping missions on its territory. This situation alone created new dimensions in the conflict.

Mediation

Owing to the ineffectiveness of the Darfur peace agreement, two special envoys were appointed by the AU and UN to lead the political process in Darfur. The efforts of Salim Ahmed Salim of the AU and Jan Eliasson representing the UN did not produce the expected all-inclusive agreement for UNAMID to police. The mission was therefore deployed without a peace agreement and the situation remained the same by the time I left Darfur. Both the AU and UN then decided to appoint a joint chief mediator in the person of Minister

Djibril Yèpène Bassolé of Burkina Faso. While Bassolé and his team worked hard in conjunction with the government of Qatar and UNAMID towards an all-inclusive agreement, the AU established a high panel on Darfur, led by the former president of South Africa, Mbeki. The panel produced its report and recommended to the AUPSC at the summit in Abuja in October 2009 that it be mandated to implement its own report. The AUPSC endorsed the proposal. We have all had enough time now to reflect on whether that process had a positive or negative impact on the political process in Darfur. Those of us engaged in running the mission in Darfur saw those fragmented initiatives as a lack of consensus on the Darfur conflict. Meanwhile, Abdul Waheed Nur, a key SLM rebel leader remained in Paris, while Dr Khalil Ibrahim of JEM moved his base from N'Djamena to Tripoli, Libya. All those signs of inconsistency have not helped the political process in Darfur.

At the time I left Darfur in May 2010, the situation was certainly better than it had been in the early years of the conflict because UNAMID had quite a substantial number of troops and police contingents on the ground. The military was at about 81 per cent, the police 76 per cent and the civilian staff about 74 per cent of anticipated strength. A census was successfully conducted in Darfur and national elections, including Darfur, took place in April 2010. It must be noted that although there were enough infantry units on the ground, critical operational equipment, especially in aviation, remained lacking. The five tactical helicopters provided by Ethiopia and delivered in March 2010 were still not performing any operational tasks by the time I ended my tour of duty. No other member of the UN/AU was at that time prepared to offer the further 13 helicopters. In the meantime, restrictions on the movement of UNAMID forces continued, and as the mission leadership tried to push ahead with its mandate, repeated fighting between government forces and mainly JEM and the Abdul Waheed faction of the SLM continued, resulting in civilian casualties. While UNAMID's joint special representative Prof. Gambari and the mediation under Djibril Bassolé tried to get civil society leaders involved in the political process, there were opposing forces regarding the very manner in which civil society representatives were selected. Fighting among IDPs in the IDP camps led to the further escalation of violence in Darfur.

Leadership Perspective

I believe that anyone who has been involved in finding a solution to the problem of Darfur will agree that it is fundamentally political. The only way to solve it is through openness and a consensus approach. The AU took the lead in the Darfur crisis and must be applauded for doing so, but to my mind the organisation has been in a dilemma in its strategic approach. The will to get involved is obvious, but the means to do so with the right approach have never been clear to me. During pledging conferences in the days of AMIS, African countries that claimed ownership of the operation contributed troops and police officers without the necessary support. Africa today still relies heavily on outside assistance to deploy troops. Likewise, the political initiatives are not clear to me. If the AU and the UN agree to establish a joint mission, to appoint a joint leadership and a joint chief mediator for the political process, both organisations should support all the processes. Is the war over in Darfur? My answer has always been that the situation in Darfur at the time of my departure was certainly not the same as it was in 2003-07, but Darfur conti-nued to be unsafe. Even today, peacekeeping troops are constantly attacked and killed and humanitarian deliveries are constantly hampered. Uncoordina-ted initiatives with too many special envoys continued to create gaps for the warring factions to take advantage of. The situation in Libya currently must be having its effects on Darfur, owing to that country being a main support base for one of the Darfur rebel movements.

The hybrid mission itself during my time was handicapped in many respects. Politically, it did not enjoy an approach agreed by the UN and AU, despite the tripartite meetings involving the UN, AU and government of Sudan. Issues discussed during those meetings remained unresolved for a very long time. UNAMID had been accused by all parties to the conflict, and often accused, of siding with the government, but from the very beginning the government of Sudan has always set the pace for the operation in Darfur. The government re-jected UNSC Resolution 1706 of 31 August 2006, which proposed a complete UN take-over. That objection was upheld. The hybrid operation stipulates a predominantly African mission, which has been interpreted in different forms and shapes even by the staff of UNAMID. The UNSC itself did not appear to have consensus on the situation in Darfur. The Darfur case is greatly com-plicated by the fact that Sudan is a country that has oil in which major world powers are interested. The comprehensive peace agreement between the North and South has since July 2011 resulted in separation of the latter as an inde-pendent state with lingering security problems. The government in Khartoum continues to dictate the pace because it is in the position to do so. The position of the international community with several special envoys remains unclear. These and many other issues make the Darfur case somewhat complex and one requiring a new approach if a solution is to be found.

Summary of Issues

Do all the above points and many others constitute too many strands for the Darfur conflict and therefore require a new approach?

a. AMIS was the predecessor of UNAMID. It was a bold step on the part of AU, but it is not clear why the AU did not from the very onset set itself a time-limit for transferring the mission to the UN, as was the case in Burundi. As it was, the mission was handicapped by *donor support*. The support was very disjointed in many ways. Communication towers were erected and equipment provided without air-time to operate them. Indeed, there was no inter-office communication during the days of AMIS. Accommodation for peacekeepers was a huge problem. There was no civilian component of the mission for a long time and the logistics nightmares were too numerous to enumerate.

b. It was precisely because of the many shortcomings that the AU in its communiqué of 12 January 2006 indicated its willingness to transfer operations to the UN. However, when the Sudanese government rejected UNSC Resolution 1706 of August 2006, the UN/AU had to return to the drawing board. The result was the 16 November 2006 high level meeting chaired by the then Secretary-General and the AU chairperson in Addis Ababa, where it was agreed that there should be a political process, ceasefire and a three step approach to peacekeeping in Darfur: the light support package, heavy support package and hybrid operation.

c. The political process, as we all know, did not and still has not produced an all-inclusive agreement. The hybrid mission was established through UNSC Resolution 1769 of 31 July 2007 without an all-inclusive peace agreement. Several special envoys were appointed for the Darfur conflict with different agendas. Who had the political mandate: the joint mediators, UN, AU or the envoys?

d. There was and there still is no ceasefire in Darfur. Peacekeeping called for the light support package and heavy support package before the takeover from AMIS. While the light support package was somehow implemented, the heavy support package never was. The latter was to provide the mission with enablers and multipliers and therefore the necessary foundation for the initiation of the hybrid operations.

e. Essentially, nothing changed on the ground in Darfur except the wearing of the UN blue beret. Even that was difficult on the day of transfer of authority on 31 December 2007. Everything logistically remained the same and the Darfur population lost confidence in the mission from the very start. We were building a failure on earlier AMIS difficulties. Indeed, was UNAMID also not looking like a donor support mission when African police contributing countries had to wait for equipment and vehicles to be provided by the developed world before formed police units could be deployed?

f. One of the modalities for the establishment of UNAMID was that it would operate under UN rules and regulations. It has never been clear to me whether the UN and AU agreed on what that statement meant. On the part of the UN, once the mission was to be financially supported from the assessed contributions of the member states, everything had to be done according to established procedures. Often, long debates, meetings upon meetings between DPKO and AUPSC could not achieve an agreed position for both organisations.

g. At times, the selection of senior leaders for the mission took a very long time.

h. Communication with the mission was a problem. New York (DPKO), far away from Darfur, was in more regular communication with the mission than Addis Ababa. Sometimes, we in Darfur wondered if anyone in Addis Ababa was dedicated to be in touch with the mission in Darfur. The establishment of the joint support coordination mechanism was intended to help, but has it been effective?

i. As a joint mission, decisions at critical times were not easy to handle and that was where the leadership had to take bold decisions to avert catastrophe.

j. UNAMID during my time did not have a humanitarian mandate and still does not have one. UNMIS, headquartered in Khartoum at the time, had the mandate even though the largest humanitarian operation in Sudan at the time was in Darfur. Coordination was a problem. It was as if the mission was set up not to work.

k. It is worth recalling the clause in Resolution 1769 which stated that the peacekeeping mission should be predominantly African. This statement was used effectively by the government of Sudan, and even senior members of UNAMID overemphasised this point, to delay the arrival of the support required for the mission. Indeed, I saw the government of Sudan, even though it is a party to the conflict, strongly in control of affairs in Darfur. Unless the government agreed on an issue, it was never implemented. If UNAMID managed to occasionally push through its decisions, they were not without consequences.

l. It is not difficult to conclude that there was a lack of unanimity on Darfur among the UNSC permanent members because of the differing interests of each country.

m. The indictment of President Bashir by the International Criminal Court and the subsequent position taken by the AU and UN on the matter strained relations between both organisations to the detriment of UNAMID.

Having enumerated the points above, were there some advantages to our operations in Darfur? Yes:

a. It was a trial test of cooperation between the UN and the AU to give practical meaning to Chapter VIII of the UN Charter;
b. Senior African leaders, troops and police had the opportunity to work together in a conflict zone and those lessons could help in educating them to work for peace in their own countries;
c. The resolve of the AU must have been tested in many respects;
d. Any future hybrid mission would certainly learn lessons from UNAMID and the basis for establishing such a mission should be clear;
e. Weaknesses in the UN's cooperation with a regional organisation, especially the AU, have been revealed.
f. The presence of UNAMID and its predecessor AMIS in Darfur has saved many lives that otherwise would have been in grave danger;
g. Both UNAMID and UNMIS create the opportunity to study of a new area of peacekeeping in a 'non-failed' state. Here is a government that is financially and politically strong with almost all state institutions in place, a government with two peacekeeping missions to handle;
h. UNAMID's presence in Darfur has reduced violence and to some extent created the opportunity and support for dialogue;
i. AU headquarters have improved telecommunication systems with the UN. Before I left Darfur, it was possible for DPKO to have a video-teleconference with AU headquarters in Addis Ababa. The UN provided and operated the facility.

There are certain issues I consider to be lost opportunities in relation to UNAMID. I have a firm belief that there are possible advantages that have been lost or can still be reaped, for example, staff training or capacity building. All the qualified AMIS staff were taken onboard as UN staff, which is financially rewarding to the individuals. They are all currently UN staff and will never return to the AU, perhaps only as consultants in the distant future. Is AU capacity in peacekeeping being built? The AU can second some of its current staff to UNAMID on a rotational basis for six months. The placements should be in both substantive sections and mission support. The AU would then learn how the UN operates in areas such as financial regulations and compliance, recruitment processes, logistical support and supply chain management, coordination with humanitarian organisations, political reporting, accountability, etc. Indeed, the original idea for absorbing AMIS personnel into UNAMID was to build capacity for the AU.

Conclusion

Personally, my views are that the UN-AU hybrid operation in Darfur has not been a bad idea. I saw it as a challenge to us African senior members of the mission and many of us who took the lead in Darfur did everything, including making great sacrifices to our health and security. But the circumstances, some of which I have enumerated, have not allowed the mission to make the desired progress. The UN and the AU certainly need a better and more concrete understanding between themselves if such a venture is to succeed. All peacekeeping missions are politically driven, and the permanent members of the UNSC and AU heads of state must have an agreed position on the Darfur conflict. Without a concrete agreement and with the Sudanese government remaining strong, the Darfur conflict will continue to torment women and children. If the world keeps on ignoring those oppressed, hungry and locked up people in IDP camps and to give credit to oppressive governments and shield rebel groups, even the rich will never live in peace. The fragmented initiatives must yield to a common position and all efforts directed to an agreed mediation process must be geared to producing an all-inclusive agreement that all the warring factions will respect. Without such an agreement and with the government of Sudan dictating the pace, any UN support system to operations in Darfur will remain ineffective.

Recommendation

My recommendation is that since there is bound to be a time lag in the deployment of UN peacekeepers, regional organisations such as the AU or its sub-regional organisations may have to continue 'to put out the fire' while preparing the ground for a full UN take-over. Firm arrangements in support of such interim solutions should be clearly spelled out. This model worked in Burundi, Sierra Leone and Liberia. In that regard, support to TCCs and PCCs by the developed world should not be a one-time measure but should be sustained, otherwise armoured personnel carriers sent to the missions will remain in garages instead of going on patrols.

4. Reflections on the AU-UN Hybrid Model in Darfur

Martin Luther Agwai

Having discussed the AMIS model and its challenges, it will be easier for us to understand some of the challenges that confronted the AU-UN hybrid operation in Darfur (UNAMID) and the model. However, before we go into that discussion, I will state upfront that the challenges that confronted the AU during AMIS days are still there and it is necessary to find adequate solutions, because the AU is expected to play a greater role in future conflict resolution in Africa. Indeed, there are still several conflict-fuelling resources in Africa and there are several states and non-state actors that are ready to provide military and financial support to local clients. Meanwhile, the current drift of the UNSC back to the Cold War days, when reaching a consensus was impossible, is making UN intervention difficult.

We live in a period when Africa has the largest and highest number of UN troops and missions and where the numbers are not going to go down, but may have to go up. The events of Côte d'Ivoire and Libya go to show that the AU may be compelled to take higher responsibility in conflict management in Africa, despite its current lack of capability.

On UNAMID, let us start by looking at the highlights of its mandate, which is based on three major points:

a. Protection of civilians.
b. Creation of the conditions to allow delivery of humanitarian aid and the voluntary return of IDPs.
c. Durable peace, security and stability in Darfur.

The UNAMID mandate states that the mission's objective is:

> to assist the Parties in implementing the Darfur Peace Agreement or any subsequent agreement, through contributing to the protection of civilians and creation of security conditions that allow unhindered access for the delivery of humanitarian aid and voluntary return of IDPs and Refugees to their homes thus enabling reconciliation and confidence building necessary for durable peace, security and stability in Darfur.

Major Challenges to UNAMID

To appreciate the challenges of UNAMID, it is necessary to look into its background. In July 2004, AMIS deployed to Darfur as an observer mission to monitor the N'Djamena humanitarian ceasefire agreement. The proposed expansion of AMIS was based on the hope that the Abuja peace agreement on Darfur was going to be signed by all the parties involved in the conflict. The drawback of the agreement was that it was signed by only one rebel leader, Minni Minawi, while JEM and the SLM of Wahid did not sign it. There were also a number of unmet demands, which ranged from the supervision of Janjaweed disarmament to more representation in each state assembly in the three Darfur states. The inability to achieve a consensus also polarised communities, particularly the IDPs, into those who favoured the agreement and those who opposed it. This was the first major challenge to UNAMID: since not all the parties had signed the peace agreement, there was no agreement in place. The second major challenge was the rejection in August 2006 by the government of Sudan of proposed UNSC Resolution 1706 calling for the deployment of 22,000 UN troops and police to support AMIS. This led to the agreement of June 2007, which later became the basis of UNSC Resolution 1769 that created UNAMID. It was based on the implementation of a light support package, a heavy support package and then the deployment of UNAMID. However, by the time of the transfer of authority from AMIS to UNAMID, the light support package was not fully implemented and the heavy support package had hardly begun. In reality, the mission started with the cart being put before the horse.

Other Challenges

Sudan at the time of UNAMID's initial deployment was the largest country in Africa. It was also in a politically unstable region, since it was bordered to the north by Egypt, to the northeast and east by Eritrea and Ethiopia, to the south by Uganda and DRC, and in the west by the Central African Republic, Chad and Libya. Darfur is largely an arid plateau made up of open desert and lush grasslands, and includes the once volcanic hills of the Jebel Mara, which rise to almost 3,000 metres. It is a vast and isolated region of Sudan, and is the size of Kenya. The Darfur region is also 2,500 kilometres from the Red Sea coast and its infrastructure, particularly roads and airports capable of taking the largest aircraft, is under-developed. This posed a very significant challenge when the AU first deployed, and it remains a challenge to UNAMID, not only for deployment but also for sustainment of the mission. It is fair to say these factors were not fully appreciated when the deployment was first conceived and when the international community may have felt pressured to act and thus did not think through all the challenges. This was one of the main reasons the deployment of the main UNAMID force and its equipment was slower than expected.

The tension between Sudan and Chad that was playing out in western Darfur was also a challenge for UNAMID. The Chadian armed opposition groups, with the support of the government of Sudan, operated out of western Darfur into Chad. They launched the audacious attack on N'Djamena in February 2008 that very nearly succeeded. On the other side, JEM uses eastern Chad as a safe haven with the support of the government of Chad. JEM mounted the even more audacious attack in May 2008 on Omdurman on the outskirts of Khartoum. It is fair to say that peace in Darfur is subject to the resolution of the wider Sudan-Chad conflict. Thus, addressing and resolving the regional dimension of the conflict involved in the Chad-Sudan proxy war was crucial to UNAMID's success but was not part of its mandate.

Nothing is ever simple in Darfur. It is necessary to have a general understanding of the players on the stage, some of whom I have already mentioned. At the beginning of the Abuja peace talks, there were two main rebel movements sitting at the negotiating table. However, before the end of the talks in 2006, there were two SLMs, one led by Minni and the other by Wahid. By 2008, there was an alphabet soup of rebel groups, each consisting of young men with machine-guns determined to fight on the battlefield rather than to take their place around the table. It might scarcely be believed but there were as many as 30 rebel factions. There was SLM-Minni, SLM-Unity, SLM-Mother, SLM-Free Will, SLM-Peace, the United Revolutionary Front, JEM, JEM-Peace, JEM-Unity, and these were just the better known ones. So UNAMID, a peacekeeping force, found itself on a battlefield that pitted government against rebels, Arab against Arab, African against African, rebel against rebel, Janjaweed against government, bandits against civilians and aid workers, all against the background of an apparent proxy war between Sudan and Chad.

Another factor unique to UNAMID is its hybrid nature, which causes it to have two masters: the AU in Addis Ababa and the UN in New York. The head of mission, instead of being special representative of the Secretary-General is referred to as the joint special representative and reports to both. When one master is so proficient in peacekeeping, it can be easy to lean too much in one direction, and an adjustment may be required to redress the balance on occasion. Conversely, it is all too easy for AU headquarters to be left out of the information loop, as the details of the deployment are organised by New York.

A further challenge was that faced by the logisticians. UNAMID has over 30 locations and routes, many of them impassable especially in the rainy season. Mi26 Halo heavy lift helicopters were key resupply tools, particularly in the wet season. Water remains a critical asset for all. These challenges did affect operations on the ground and led to some lack of flexibility in the deployment and employment of troops. The lack of specialist assets that ranged from key enablers, such as engineers, transport and logistics units, to more specialised force multipliers, such as utility and attack helicopters and fixed-wing surveillance aircraft, did affect the ability of the force to operate by day and by night. The original plan was that the enablers should deploy first. The former AMIS battalions would then be reinforced and the eight new battalions would subsequently deploy. The reality was not so simple: years later, enablers and battalions were arriving together and no TCCS had yet been identified for many of the key assets, particularly utility helicopters.

Mandate Implementation

At the same time, of course, UNAMID was endeavouring to fulfil its mission, key parts of which were the protection of civilians, creation of the conditions to allow for the delivery of humanitarian aid and the voluntary return of IDPs and refugees. The mission is a Chapter VII mission, but it is also very much a humanitarian one. The protection teams comprising military, police and civilians go out each day in an effort to provide the stability that is so desperately required. Some missions are confidence-building and aimed at providing a reassuring presence while others are more mundane firewood patrols to provide security to the women who go out to collect firewood and who might otherwise be raped. Hearts and minds was a phrase that we all recognised: it is often the most mundane acts that can generate the most goodwill. These teams intervened on a daily basis across the length and breadth of Darfur to calm tensions arising from cattle losses, water distribution and land ownership, issues that lie at the heart of the Darfur conflict. These missions are critical, successful and welcomed by the local people. Although they do not make international headlines, please be in no doubt of their importance to the people the mission was there to protect. In terms of the humanitarian effort, UNAMID works with colleagues in sister organisations and other agencies to ensure that the needs of IDPs and others are met.

UNAMID engages the parties to the conflict on a daily basis. It meets regularly with the government of Sudan at the highest level, engages with regional leaders in the three states of Darfur and talks to rebel movements on an ongoing basis. In theory, there is an agreement among all parties that there can be no military solution to this conflict. Only a political settlement can bring an end to this war. Nevertheless, with the best will in the world, when you have 30 rebel movements and a government unwilling or unable to make a compromise, there is little pay-back or progress.

Lessons Learned From UNAMID

We should not underestimate the difficulties facing UNAMID. Remember that when the AU first deployed its forces to Darfur in July 2004, it became clear that few countries in Africa had the equipment to conduct expeditionary operations. Most AMIS units had to rely on donors to provide much of their equipment. For example, Canada provided Grizzly armoured personnel carriers and air support; the UK and the EU provided communication equipment and allowances; while the US provided accommodation and food supplies for the mission. However, when providing such assistance, the equipment should have spare parts back-up and the relevant support training should be provided for the repair team. This was the first hybrid mission, a partnership between the AU and UN. The AU and its contributing nations showed that they were not yet sufficiently mature to generate, train, deploy and sustain a mission of this size and to provide the headquarters staff to command it. UNAMID is largely African. In the long run, it is hoped this experiment and the lessons learned from the operation will improve future coordination and control between the UN and regional organisations and also be a source of capacity building for the AU and its standby forces.

There are lessons to be learned for the AU. UNAMID was a breathtakingly ambitious deployment and it has shown how much both experience and the right equipment are needed if the mission is to succeed. The AU has the trump card of soldiers that can be deployed in large numbers quickly, but it does not have the financial capacity of the UN. However, there are often circumstances when a rapid if lightly armed deployment can have a decisive effect on the ground, but there needs to be a follow-on plan to sustain the original deployment. The UN is a supertanker of an organisation: it can be slow to get going but is invariably impressive when it is up and running, as in the cases of Liberia, Côte d'Ivoire and Burundi, where the African forces paved the way and the UN then followed.

AU and Peace Support Operations in Africa

The major powers, especially the permanent members of the UNSC, do tend to dictate where and when the UN missions are deployed and for how long. There is a need for the AUPSC to work closely with the UNSC and, if need be, to lobby neutral countries such as Sweden, other Nordic countries, other regional organisations and powers to push the permanent UNSC members to be more even-handed in mandating peacekeeping missions in Africa or to help provide resources for the AU to effectively undertake missions, for example in Somalia. Having the support of 'sponsors' such as the US, UK, France, Russia and China in their historical spheres of influence is a critical factor. The UN Mission in Sierra Leone and UN Operation in Côte d'Ivoire were deployed even in the face of major setbacks because of the support they got from UK and France respectively, which may be due to the colonial heritage. The UN Mission in Liberia (UNMIL) is supported by the US based on historical ties and Cold War alliance. Russia played a major role in bringing their former Marxist allies Mozambique and Angola to the negotiating table and to the deployment of the UN operation in Mozambique and the UN Angola verification mission. Without the push from China, it may have been difficult for Sudan to accept the deployment of UNAMID.

For peace support to be effective and successful, there is a need for national, regional and international powers to work together. I saw this working in Sierra Leone during my service in UNAMSIL as a deputy force commander. At the national level, the willingness of belligerent parties, particularly the Revolutionary United Front under Issa Sesay, to cooperate with UNAMSIL to implement ceasefire accords was critical and it made our strategy to deal with potential spoilers unnecessary. ECOWAS as a regional body also played a leading role in achieving peace in Sierra Leone. It contributed troops and police to UNAMSIL, organised several ceasefire negotiations and provided the Kabbah administration with diplomatic support, especially during the disarmament of the RUF rebels and the civil defence force. It was only by achieving a degree of consensus at all three interdependent levels that UNAMSIL became a successful peacekeeping mission. All three levels are interconnected, and without multi-level commitment it would have proven difficult for UNAMSIL to achieve successful disarmament, demobilisation and reintegration and peace in Sierra Leone. In the absence of involvement by international powers and ECOWAS, the healing of sub-regional divisions would have been difficult and UNAMSIL interventions would have lacked sub-regional legitimacy. The RUF might have continued to enjoy support from some regional or external states. And without external support from international powers, particularly the permanent UNSC members, UN peacekeeping often lacked resources and military effectiveness. The permanent members of the UNSC, with the UK and the US in the lead, did mobilise diplomatic and financial support for the mission. They worked to ensure the consent of domestic parties in implementing the ceasefire agreement and developed incentives for cooperation by RUF rebels and countries in the region. They also imposed sanctions for noncompliance by applying diplomatic or economic pressure.

There is a need for the AU to establish and build a strong humanitarian community with a proper grasp of the important domestic and regional intricacies of Africa that turn IDPs and refugees into hostages in the camps. To achieve the required synergy, all those who participate in peace support operations must be professionally trained. Besides the capacity training that continental and regional centres provide, member states should be encouraged to continue training their personnel and to provide refresher training where necessary. They should be gender sensitive in their recruitment and retention of peacekeepers.

I have gone to some lengths in describing what happened in UNAMID because of my concern about which model we should accept for future international assistance to the AU in peace support operations in Africa. Whatever model is accepted, there is a need to fully consider the challenges. I make some suggestions because conflicts will continue to dominate a large part of Africa in the next decade or so. Natural resources have played a major role in most former African conflicts and there are still strategic minerals in parts of Africa where there is a lack of democracy and corrupt governments. Given these challenges, the international community should remain engaged with the AU in conflict resolution in Africa.

Lack of Military Capabilities among African Contingents

As we have seen, Africa's experience in various UN operations and Western-led multinational missions is vast, but underscores the problems encountered when the continent undertakes missions on its own. African countries contributing formed units to these missions have tended to provide infantry battalions with modest assets. Only a few African countries have been able to provide specialised units to such undertakings. Many countries are willing to deploy troops in UN and non-UN operations, but the absence of financial and logistical support severely undermines the ability of those troops to function effectively. It follows, then, that many of the difficulties African organisations and *ad hoc* coalitions have encountered when fielding their own forces relate to the military capabilities of participating states. Only a few African countries are capable of deploying a battalion for a peacekeeping operation or multinational force without significant assistance. In addition, most do not possess specialised units with sufficient equipment or expertise to provide such services as engineering, communications, medical or movement control. African countries whose militaries do possess some of these skills are hard-pressed to make them available for extended periods. With few exceptions, African countries cannot project force over great distances with the desired level of self-sufficiency. The ability to sustain a sizeable force presents a more significant obstacle.

Lack of Specialised Contingents to Serve Within Regional Peacekeeping Forces

From experience, the AU and its regional organisation need UN assistance and support for their peacekeeping initiatives in areas that they are weak (for example, specialised units that with effective support can act as a force multiplier). The intelligence requirements in support of peacekeeping operations are supposed to be similar in nature to those required during major operations, if not much larger (by volume). Intelligence is supposed to provide the assessments that will help the military leadership to decide which forces to deploy, when, how and where as well as how to employ them in a manner that accomplishes the mission. Intelligence is essential to force protection and provides indications and warnings. A well-equipped and well-trained signals unit would be an especially welcome addition to AU operations, given that such initiatives often lack reliable communication links between headquarters and contingent or sector commands. Similarly, a well-equipped logistics unit would also be helpful in light of the operational shortcomings that African troops face. The command structure of the force would potentially be a delicate issue, which should be addressed prior to the force's deployment. The UN and other partners would need to make a much better investment by supporting the formed units instead of concentrating on military observers, and to create a more symbiotic relationship with the AU by assisting in meeting the AU's identified challenges.

Conclusion

The assertion that the UN cannot address every potential and actual conflict is correct and necessitates the existence of a burden-sharing mechanism whe-

reby the AU can assist the world body, particularly in Africa. Africa has shown political will in Liberia, Côte d'Ivoire and recently in Darfur but because Africa's economies and institutions are weak there is a need for the UNSC to find sustainable ways to provide adequate funds and resources to the AU for peace support operations in Africa. There should be capacity building for the military, police and civilians. There is a need to assist the AU and its member states in identified areas where they are weak or lack capacity. From recent operations, particularly the Darfur experience, it is clear that the military will need specialised units – engineering, transport, medical and logistics – and specialised force multipliers – intelligence and communication. As for civilians, there is a need for those who can manage a mission, especially those who can participate in humanitarian activities.

Current efforts by several partners working with the AU to develop African peace support capacities are laudable and provide a basis upon which to build. There is an overriding need for the UN and other institutions to reassert themselves in peacekeeping in Africa, knowing that peace in Africa means peace in the world.

5. Joint and Integrated AU-UN Mediation in Darfur: A Model for Future African Peace Processes?

Cage Banseka

Historical background

The present peace process in Darfur was necessitated by the failure of the Abuja agreement of May 2006 to bring about a definite end to the conflict in the region and to usher in a period of sustainable stability and development. Not only was it a partially signed agreement, but even those who signed it found it extremely difficult to implement, especially given the compulsion under which they signed. Those who did not sign the agreement (Abdel Wahid al Nur faction of the SLM and JEM) were the ones who first descended on the field to introduce it to the Darfurians. Of course, they preached that the document was heresy and before those who signed and were supposed to implement it could arrive, the fate of the Darfur peace agreement had been sealed. There was a general rejection of the agreement, made worse by the failure of the rebel movements to take a concerted stance on the way forward. The period after the signing of the agreement therefore saw a serious splintering of the movements, which transformed the security landscape in Darfur into a real nightmare, a situation that would soon oblige the international community to seek another round of peace talks.

This paper seeks to explore the nature of the AU and UN hybrid/joint operations in peacemaking in Africa, and whether the present experiences of hybrid mechanisms and UN support to the AU will become a model for the future. It analyses the issue of 'jointness' in a bid to also understand whether these UN support models afforded to the AU have made a fundamental difference; whether they are feasible and desirable; and also whether AU and UN efforts under their present organisational culture, approach, vision and *modus operandi* are compatible with the search for peace in Africa. To this end, the paper examines some of the difficulties faced in the peace talks in Abuja that precipitated the introduction of hybrid/joint mediation in an attempt to find a definite solution to the crisis. The paper then explores what the hydra-headed, joint mediation could have done better under the prevailing circumstances, and the advantages and disadvantages of joint mediation.

Shortcomings of Abuja Talks and the Precursor to Joint Mediation

The Abuja process, especially the seventh round, faced serious problems that would eventually make future mediations rather difficult. The main challenges included:

- The government of Sudan and rebels were not willing to cooperate with each other, preferring instead to seek defeat of the opponent.
- The government of Sudan and rebels were not willing to engage in serious negotiations or to make concessions.
- The parties did not show respect for each other and used inappropriate language in talking to or describing each other.
- The divisions among the rebel groups inhibited progress. The rebels spent more time negotiating with each other than with the government.
- The parties tried to negotiate with the mediators and the media rather than with each other, while hoping that the mediators would eventually find a solution to their problems.
- The rebels did not have a clearly worked out position on security and how to deal with their own internal security issues.
- The negotiations in Abuja were purely a government of Sudan-rebel affair and did not involve civil society in Darfur or the diaspora.

Another set of challenges was closely linked to international actors. Indeed, the government of Sudan appeared to be making concessions more in response to the views of the international community than to the Darfurians. This was prompted by the presence of Robert Zoellick and Hilary Benn, who brought much pressure to bear on the rebels, to which Minni Minawi, the lone signatory, succumbed. He joined the government of Sudan, but lacked the necessary acumen and brinkmanship to survive the murky politics in Khartoum. The international community also did not give him the assistance, guidance and political orientation he needed so direly, and allowed him to join the government of Sudan with plenty of misperceptions, poor calculations, false hopes and unjustified expectations. Minni Minawi finally succumbed under the weight of his own miscalculation, political incompetence and the asymmetrical relationship with the government of Sudan in Khartoum. The difficulties he faced after the signing of the Darfur peace agreement brought implementation of the agreement to a standstill, while the security situation in Darfur continued to deteriorate, forcing both Darfurians and the international community into another painful period of soul-searching. It is against this backdrop that the international community decided to initiate another peace process, this one hydra-headed and involving mediators appointed by the AU and UN.

AU-UN Joint Mediation

The AU-UN joint mediation support team was created by the UNSC and AUPSC towards the end of 2006 with the intention of capitalising on the spirit of cooperation and common purpose regarding the Darfur crisis. It was headed by veteran Tanzanian politician and chief negotiator of the Abuja talks, Salim Ahmed Salim, and the former foreign minister of Sweden, Jan Eliasson. The proven pragmatism of these officials and their prior experience need no defending here, although the mediation team had to spend many months trying to make Salim Salim an acceptable mediator in the eyes of the rebels. He had been discredited over his performance in Abuja and the rebels saw him as representing an AU that did not appear to be a neutral and honest arbiter in the Darfur peace process. However, both officials had the added advantage of great comprehension of international mediation contexts. Their support team was composed of former AMIS and other AU officers and staff from the UN. The mediators embarked on their assignment based on a three point roadmap:

1. Bring all other initiatives on the Darfur peace process under the umbrella of the joint mediation support team;
2. Unify the splintered rebel movements;
3. Start substantive talks.

The integration of civil society into the talks as a structural and methodological requirement was also a basic objective of the mediators, though it was not included in the roadmap. Through this roadmap, the mediators foresaw a swift and expeditious end to the crisis and the signing of an agreement, especially as the UN side brought with it requisite finances and met the precondition of having Westerners at the negotiations, which the rebel factions in Abuja had been demanding.

Apart from following their roadmap, the mediators also assessed the strengths and weaknesses of the Darfur peace agreement and of the parties in negotiating agreements and how to enhance these skills. In their interactions with the parties, they explained that they could not get what they wanted by unilateral action and that even in the most hostile situations there would be interdependence between them. The constant fighting they were involved in only made sense if it was followed by peaceful negotiations and an agreement that would provide better opportunities for Darfurians, especially the ability to meet basic livelihood needs and individual, social, economic, political security and protection, including justice and human rights. This would entail the preservation of individual, cultural and religious identity and other basic values.

The mediators also explored the operational and strategic aspects of the confrontation between the government of Sudan and the rebels; what incentives the parties were responding to; what choices they had; what their alternatives were; how they viewed the strategy and behaviour of the other parties; and why eventually they might hesitate to engage each other honestly in negotiations. All of these explorations were meant to support an orientation to the future among the parties; show respect for all individuals involved; and give them reason to be open and to seek common ground in negotiations that all could accept.

Unification of Movements in Juba and Internal Cracks in the Joint Mediation

Unifying the splintered rebel movements, especially the SLM/A, prior to the talks was an exigency for the mediators. This initiative was outsourced to the Sudan People's Liberation Movement in Southern Sudan. It organised a unification conference under the auspices of the president of the then semi-autonomous southern region of Sudan and invited all the factions considered relevant. Special funding was sought by the SPLM from the international community for this initiative. The joint mediation support team maintained a permanent presence during the deliberations of the movements and their attempts at creating or recreating alliances. The team sent daily reports, assessments, analyses and opinions to the principals for their consideration.

The SPLM was chosen for this project based on its own experience of rebellion and also of the constant splintering of forces in the course thereof. It could also empathise with the Darfur rebel movements, given its own rebellion against Khartoum. The authorities of the south were therefore keen to prove their negotiation prowess and contribute to pacification of the restive western part of the country. However, SPLM also used the unification process to secure a political in into Darfur and eventually hijacked the process to its own ends. It demonstrated unwillingness to allow rebel elements to join the talks in Sirte, and was determined to use the newfound alliances with them against the central government in Khartoum.

Despite the initial goodwill of the SPLM, the determination of the mediators and international community interest in this project, the unification process bore little fruit and was for all intents and purposes a failure. The rebel factions were not ready to either unite under one faction or unify their positions prior to coming to the already organised negotiations with the government of Sudan in Sirte, Libya. Contested leadership, misperceptions and miscalculations, grandstanding and the inability to submit themselves to the others meant that the rebel factions were at daggers drawn. Additionally, some of the most important factions did not attend the Juba conference and were unwilling to be part of the negotiations.

It was under these circumstances that some joint mediation support team staff present in Juba began to express reservations about the prospects of the conference. Some went ahead to recommend that the start of the Sirte process be postponed or that it be organised as a low-key event. They argued for pragmatism over rigid adherence to dates and deadlines, and this plunged the so-called AU and UN sides into tense confrontations. It was equally on this point that the first major cracks began to appear in the mediation team itself, with AU staff insisting on postponing Sirte, not sending out invitations to the movements to participate, and not organising a grand opening ceremony for the talks, in the event the principals decided to go ahead with them.

Jan Eliasson and others from the UN insisted on the start of talks, which they saw as ending on 31 December 2007 with the signing of a peace agreement and prior to the start of the mandate of the newly created UNAMID. Eliasson kept repeating his famous slogan that the train had left the station and would no longer stop. He subtly expressed abhorrence at the wait and see mentality he saw as characterising the AU approach. This infuriated some of the staff from the so-called AU side.

Sirte Peace Process: Final Straw and Collapse of Mediation and Peace Talks

The peace process that begun in Sirte in September 2007 was born crippled. First, only very few of the rebel factions attended (17 of the 134 present in Juba). Second, the cracks in the mediation team itself had widened leading to more internal divisions on issues of procedure, timing and recruitment and many conspiracy theories. Both sides started holding separate meetings, taking separate decisions and sending different reports to their respective headquarters. However, in public the principals exhibited political maturity and insisted on continuation of their newfound brotherhood.

The opening ceremony of the Sirte talks was full of pomp and pageantry, contrary to the wish and design of the AU side. The meagre presence of the rebel movements at this event made such hype even more ridiculous. The statement by the late President Gaddafi that the conflict in Darfur was just like a fight over a camel between two neighbours and did not necessitate such huge international attention and presence, had a further crippling effect on the Sirte talks from their very outset.

Several meetings were held after the opening ceremony, but it had become increasingly clear that the Sirte process was heading towards failure and premature ending, with the expectation of an agreement by 31 December becoming ever more fanciful. It was under these circumstances that both Eliasson and Salim ended their tenures as mediators in the Darfur conflict. To argue that it was the advent of the UN to the mediation scene that led to this failure might be too simplistic. The basic objective of the AU and UN and the two mediators was the search for peace in Darfur. However, the inability of the rebel factions to unite or coordinate their negotiating positions would have baffled even the most gifted politicians.

Nomination of a Single Mediator: Djibrill Bassolé

The hydra-headed mediation of Eliasson and Salim, which started with so much euphoria, ended on a low note. It is under these circumstances that a single joint chief mediator was named by the AU and UN. Unlike his predecessors, Djibrill Bassolé had to be resident in Sudan. He took over his duties at the time the International Criminal Court decided to issue an arrest warrant for President Al-Bashir, so from the outset he faced a major hurdle. However, the joint chief mediator decided to remain completely neutral on the arrest issue.

He conducted wide consultations in Sudan and in the region. He met and established regular contacts with government of Sudan authorities and rebel factions. He also made contact with other major actors and stakeholders in the international community, a demarche for which he would be later vehemently criticised by the AU, which claimed he paid more attention to international partners at the expense of the AUPSC and AU Commission.

During Bassolé's tenure, the AU, UN and League of Arab States decided on Doha, Qatar as the venue for the negotiations. After several initial rounds of consultation, the joint chief mediator invited the government of Sudan and rebel factions to start direct talks in Doha. It was here that JEM and the government of Sudan signed a goodwill agreement in February 2009 and the framework and cessation of hostilities agreements in February 2010. It was equally in Doha that framework and cessation agreements were signed between the government of Sudan and the LJM in March 2010, and eventually the Doha Document for Peace in Darfur in July 2011, after intensive negotiations. JEM did not sign the latter agreement, preferring to think it did not yet fully meet the aspirations of the Darfur people.

The joint chief mediator and the state of Qatar also organised two civil society forums, a conference for IDPs and refugees and finally an all Darfur stakeholders conference in Doha. These events were attended by several hundreds of people from Darfur, Sudan and the international community.

In the meantime and in the lead up to the signing of these agreements, the joint chief mediator continued his intense shuttle diplomacy in an attempt to convince all the holdout movements to join the talks. He never gave up on them despite their many broken promises to attend the talks. The rebel factions continued insisting on one precondition after another despite the persuasion and constant appeals of the AU, UN, League of Arab States and other partners in the international community. The holdout movements, especially JEM and the Abdel Wahid al Nur faction of the SLM have till today not genuinely engaged the government of Sudan on the political process, preferring to join other alliances seeking to topple the government in Khartoum by military means. LJM, for its part, has signed the Doha Document for Peace in Darfur and has joined the government of Sudan in efforts to implement it in Darfur and to pacify the region. The signing of the Doha document also saw the departure of the Bassolé from the peace process and the nomination of Ibrahim Gambari, current head of UNAMID, as the new joint chief mediator.

Assessment of 'Jointness' in the Salim-Eliasson Mediation

The international shift in focus from single (AU) to joint (AU-UN) mediation was meant to mirror international community concern about the crisis in Darfur and its victims. However, competing advocacies made this joint mediation imprecise and ambiguous, leading some onlookers to develop doubts about the desired outcomes. Not only did the initial rejection of Salim Salim constrain progress, but several factors militated against 'jointness' in the hydra-headed Salim-Eliasson proces . These factors included:

- **Inability to develop a common calendar for activities on the ground**: Despite their claimed unity of purpose in a common endeavour, Salim and Eliasson often found it difficult to synchronise the calendar of activities for the peace process. This often led to the two officials visiting Sudan and Darfur at different times and officiating at different meetings. The dangers of contradiction, duplication and differing and confusing signals to the parties became real.

- **Living in different locations**: The two mediators were not resident in Sudan, and were therefore far removed from the daily realities of the perpetrators and victims of the war. Their presence in Sudan was most often on a tight schedule and this limited any meaningful accomplishments during these trips.
- **Differences in approach**: The insistence of the AU and government of Sudan that the conflict in Darfur was an African conflict requiring African solutions made for different approaches by the two mediators and impacted their *modus operandi*. The approaches of Eliasson were interpreted as Western and foreign, and many saw him as a representative of Western interests in the conflict in Darfur. Much cynicism crept into the process as a result of this view.
- **Different levels of experience in Darfur Mediation**: The fact that Salim had negotiated the Darfur peace agreement gave him a certain leverage on the Darfur file, while many considered Eliasson a novice on the issue. Ironically, a feeling developed in relation to the mediation that the UN had come in to right the wrongs of the AU committed during the Darfur peace agreement negotiations and which eventually led to its failure. The AU side of the team interpreted this as arrogance, and this was to lead further cracks in relations between the two sides.
- **Differences in organisational cultures**: The AU approach to conflict resolution tends to be more ethnocentric, while the UN has developed different mechanisms for resolving differences. The feeling often crept into the AU that the failure to resolve African conflicts has been due to undue Western interventionism in the continent's crises. To some, the idea of joint mediation contradicted the view of an influential AU ready to take up its responsibilities in conflict resolution and preferring to look inwards. These differences could give rise to many obstacles.
- **Perceptions and prejudices**: As mentioned above, the advent of the UN to the peace process in Darfur was perceived as a way of getting right what the AU had got wrong in Abuja. The failure of the Darfur peace agreement lent some credibility to this feeling and accentuated the view that unless the UN intervened, a definitive solution would be hard to achieve. This feeling ran through the daily work of the mediation team, causing further friction. The UN side also insinuated that the only interest AU authorities had in the mediation at this point was the placement of some individuals in posts they did not deserve. This perception again widened cracks in the team, hindering internal cohesion and leading to antagonism in personal relations among the cadres.

Assessment of 'jointness' in the Bassolé Mediation

In light of the limitations and failures of the Salim-Eliasson mediation, a new mediator was appointed. The new model of 'jointness' was not much more successful than its predecessor, but important lessons can be learnt for future AU-UN collaboration in peacemaking. The major obstacles faced by Bassolé included:

- **Differences in approach by AU-UN**: The stated objective of both the AU and UN is a lasting solution to the conflict in Darfur. The nomination of a single mediator by both bodies was an attempt to avoid some of the difficulties faced by Salim and Eliasson. Despite being alone in this post, Bassolé faced his own peculiar problems linked to the different approaches of the two organisations. He assumed his duties at the same time as the Sudanese president was being indicted by the International Criminal Court with the support of the UN and much vehement opposition from the AU. Apart from exercising the neutrality of a mediator, Bassolé equally had to walk a fine line on this controversial issue, which pushed relations between the AU and UN to an all-time low. Heavily criticised by the AU for paying more attention to the UN and Western side, Bassolé was to admit later that the International Criminal Court issue marked one of his greatest challenges as joint chief mediator.

- **Duplication of assignments by AU through panels on Darfur**: Despite having named a joint chief mediator for Darfur, the AU also later created a panel for Darfur, which, in its words, represented the AU's vision for Sudan and Darfur. While the AU retains the right to articulate its vision through any form of policy mechanism, in this case the action meant the joint nomination with the UN did not fully represent the AU vision. The decision to create this panel not only raised questions about the 'jointness' of hybrid negotiations, but also created operational confusion: for instance, the Mbeki panel claimed that the joint chief mediator was supposed to report to it. Failure to do so came to be considered as spiting the AU, a view that offended many in the AU Commission. The joint chief mediator came under further heavy criticism, which distracted him from the work at hand.

- **Dependence on UNAMID for technical assistance**: Despite its multi-million dollar trust fund, the mediation was dependent on UNAMID for its financial and administrative operations. Delays in disbursing funds for activities, recruiting or paying consultants from the trust fund became a source of friction between UNAMID mission support and the mediation, leading many to think that this was a deliberate attempt to frustrate the activities of the mediator. However, relations at the political level, between the joint chief mediator and joint special representative remained very cordial.

- **Negative perceptions and prejudice:** As earlier mentioned, the joint chief mediator was perceived as leaning more towards the UN and Western powers in implementing his mandate. He was equally seen as affording the Qatari hosts an undue place at the mediation table. Moreover, he was seen as uncooperative and as constraining progress in the implementation of AU panel decisions in Darfur, especially the Darfur political process. He responded that this was merely a question of sequencing activities, but the AU and the panel continued to consider him as a negative influence on the progress of the Darfur-based political process. This impression was to remain until the departure of the joint chief mediator.

Conclusion: Joint/Hybrid AU-UN Mediation: A Model for future Peace Processes in Africa?

At face value, the evidence presented in this debate on the future of AU-UN hybrid peacekeeping and peacemaking operations in Africa seems to support the view that contemporary models are not working. However, the difficulty of finding proof for this makes it difficult to answer the question on whether AU-UN hybrid peacekeeping and peacemaking should become a model for the future definitively. It could be argued that AMIS, UNAMID and AMISOM are relatively new phenomena and that the associated policies of the AU and UN are still undergoing a litmus test. It might therefore be premature to reach a definite conclusion on the future of hybrid operations in Africa and the workability of current support models. It is interesting, however, to consider whether the present experiences will lead to changes in either side's peacekeeping and peacemaking policy, vision and *modus operandi* or lead to a hardening of positions about ownership principles, organisational culture and approaches and their relevance to the African context.

There is no doubt that, faced with incessant ordeals, both the AU and UN will feel responsible for ensuring peace and stability on the continent, but whose *modus operandi* takes precedence and why? What are the determinants of success offered by both organisations? What is their level of experience in peacekeeping and peacemaking? What is their understanding of and empathy for local realities that will ensure success? Does the mere ability to fund these activities make a difference?

The AU and UN, despite their shared conviction about the need for peace and stability, have different perceptions about how to proceed in the African context. The heads of any hybrid operations would still need to play a balancing act among the AU, UN and those at the receiving end of the mission's actions. Each will attempt to influence events in its favour and this can become potentially destabilising, especially if the head of mission becomes dependent on the good opinion of these groups for his survival. This can divert attention from the essentials of the mission and open the door to negative encroachments and disruption of activities, to the detriment of the achievement of the support project's formidable objectives.

All idealism notwithstanding, the AU and UN have different political and financial stamina, and there is a need to recognise this reality. In the UN, the opinion of rich and powerful countries can take precedence and influence policy, leading to 'controversial' decisions such as the issuance of arrest warrants for African heads of state, a stance the AU considers selective and counterproductive to peacekeeping and peacemaking on the continent. Partnership between the AU and UN under these circumstances might lead to an awkward situation 'where the strong do what they have the power to do, and the weak accept what they have to accept'.

While hybrid operations and current peacekeeping and peacemaking support models may be worth pursuing, despite the negative experiences, such models will only work if both organisations wield considerable political and financial power, and have the same vision and *modus operandi,* and if they are able to deal with one another in an equitable, open and respectful way. As long as there are competing ideologies and each seeks to push its own agenda and insist that its vision should prevail; as long as there is not enough flexibility on the part of both organisations; and as long as the AU does not have the money and human resources for self-help, the hybrid concept and contemporary support models might come to have more ingredients for failure than success.

Joint mediation thus needs reassessment and rethinking before it can be considered a future model for peacemaking in Africa.

6. Experiences of UN Support Models for AU Peace-Support Operations: The Case of the AU Mission in Somalia

James Gadin

Origin of the UN Support to AMISOM

The AUPSC, at the end of its 69th meeting on 19 January 2007, authorised the deployment of the AU Mission in Somalia, initially for six months. It was to have an authorised strength of 8,000 military personnel, 270 civilian police and a civilian component. On 20 February 2007, the UNSC adopted Resolution 1744 endorsing the deployment of AMISOM and authorising AMISOM to take 'all necessary measures' to support dialogue and reconciliation in Somalia and provide protection to the transitional federal institutions and security for key infrastructure. In addition, it was to assist with the effective re-establishment and training of all-inclusive Somali security forces and contribute to the creation of the necessary security conditions for the provision of humanitarian assistance.

Following the UNSC's authorisation of AMISOM's deployment, the AU requested the UN by a *note verbale* dated 6 March 2007 to assign planners to support the planning and preparations for the deployment of AMISOM. On 27 April 2007, the advisory committee on administrative and budgetary questions approved the deployment of 10 planners based on UNSC Resolution 1744 (2007). In June of that year, the UN planning team was deployed to the AU Commission to provide technical and expert advice on planning and managing AMISOM. Also, in a letter to the UN Secretary-General dated 20 February 2008, former AU Commission chair, Alpha Oumar Konaré, requested the UN to provide the AU with a logistical support package totalling $817 million to complete AMISOM's deployment.

In his response dated 23 April 2008, the UN Secretary-General proposed possible UN assistance to AMISOM based on two principles. First, UN support would be geared to assisting the AU build its institutional capacity to support AMISOM. Second, that AMISOM should deploy to the extent possible on the basis of UN standards to allow for the most effective 'blue-hatting' of the mission, should the UNSC decide to establish a UN peacekeeping operation in Somalia. The UN Secretary-General's proposals included provision of additional planners to the UN planning team in Addis Ababa in the areas of engineering, contract management, security, information and communications technology, logistics, contingent-owned equipment, force generation and procurement. Consequently, on 26 June 2008, the advisory committee on administrative and budgetary questions approved the deployment of 19 planners based on UNSC Resolution 1772 (2008).

Following Article 7(a) of the Djibouti agreement, which called for the deployment of an international/multinational stabilisation force, the UN Secretary-General as directed by the UNSC approached member states requesting them to contribute the required financial resources, personnel, equipment and services. However, he informed the UNSC on 16 December 2008 that of 50 countries approached, 14 had acknowledged his request and only two had offered support and/or funding. In view of this, the UN Secretary-General subsequently offered to make alternative proposals to the UNSC.

On 19 December 2008, these were submitted to the UNSC, including provision of a logistics support package to AMISOM funded from the UN assessed peacekeeping budget, and support for building the capacity of Somali rule of law and security institutions. He noted that the logistics package would include equipment and services normally provided to peacekeeping missions as UN-owned equipment and aimed to provide mission support to AMISOM to raise its operational standards.

Consequently, on 16 January 2009 the UNSC adopted Resolution 1863 expressing its intent to establish a UN peacekeeping operation in Somalia as a follow-on force to AMISOM, subject to a further decision of the Council. The resolution also approved the recommendations in the UN Secretary-General's letter of 19 December 2008, including immediate in-kind enhancement of AMISOM through the transfer of assets following the liquidation of the UN Mission in Ethiopia and Eritrea, and the provision of UN logistics equipment and services described in the UN Secretary-General's letter, but not including a transfer of funds to AMISOM.

Pursuant to Resolution 1863 (2009), the UN Support Office for AMISOM was established to deliver the logistical support to AMISOM. To facilitate effective delivery on the ground by UNSOA, a memorandum of understanding was signed between the AU Commission and the UN Secretariat in March 2009. In the meantime, the AU and the individual TCCs (Burundi and Uganda) continued to receive support from partners, particularly Algeria, the UK and the US mainly in terms of strategic airlift, training, equipment and sustenance, including troop allowances. In addition, the EU has since

2007 been the largest single financial supporter of AMISOM, providing a total of €258/$347 million through the African Peace Facility (APF) for the overhead and operational costs of AMISOM civilian, police and military personnel.

UN Support for AMISOM (UNSOA)

From the foregoing, international, in particular UN, support architecture to the AU with regard to the planning, deployment and management of AMISOM falls into three broad areas:

a. Institutional capacity building and technical advice by the UN to the AU to plan, deploy and manage AMISOM;
b. Provision and delivery of logistical support to AMISOM by the UN,
c. Voluntary financial and in-kind support to the AU and TCCs to AMISOM through various bilateral partners and institutions.

When we consider this support and funding architecture to support the AU in planning, deploying and managing AMISOM, it is, to say the least, complex and far removed from what obtains with missions mandated by the UNSC. The architecture is built on two financing systems: an assured financial system, which is the assessed budget of the UN, and an unpredictable, voluntary financial system.

I will discuss each of these support elements and then delve briefly into the support gaps, which are now being plugged by other means, including the trust fund in support of AMISOM, EU support through the APF and bilateral support from the US and a couple of EU member states either through the AU or to TCCs. In the following paragraphs I attempt to unravel this complexity and discuss whether this complex design is deliberate or the creature of circumstance.

Institutional capacity building and support to the AU for planning, deploying and managing AMISOM by UN planning team in UNOAU

Since its assignment to the AU Commission in July 2007, the UN planning team, which since July 2010 has been integrated into UNOAU, has continued to provide strategic, technical and operational advice and assistance to AUPSOD, including its plans and operations unit (formerly strategic planning and management unit), in support of AMISOM. At the request of the

AU in 2009, the planning team was reconfigured and comprises 14 planners covering military and police planning; force generation; aviation; medical; disarmament, demobilisation and reintegration; security; public information; human resources; procurement; budget; contingent-owned equipment; and information and communication technology.

Within the peace and security department at the AU Commission, AUP-SOD is the established entity responsible for the planning, deployment and management of AU-mandated peace support operations. It is the equivalent of the UN's DPKO, from which a number of the UN planners are drawn. AUPSOD's operations and plans unit is supposed to have 56 planners, but is presently not fully manned. The problem therefore is that there are no AU counterparts in some sectors to allow for active engagement and capacity buil-ding between the AU and UN as intended.

UNSOA's delivery of UN logistical support to AMISOM as authorised by UNSC Resolution 1863 (2009)

Resolution 1863 broke new ground as the UNSC agreed for the first time to fund a peacekeeping operation led by a regional organisation. The delivery of the logistics support package through UNSOA has resulted in significant improvements in AMISOM's operational capability as well as in living and working conditions for AMISOM personnel. The mandate of UNSOA was recently renewed in Resolution 2010 (2011). In addition, the UNSC decided in Resolution 1910 to include public information support in the logistical support package, thereby extending UN-assessed funding to cover costly pu-blic information operations.

Since its establishment, UNSOA has been working to provide mission support to AMISOM with a view to raising basic operational standards. Support currently provided to AMISOM includes information support ope-rations; facilities and engineering; health and sanitation; medical; commu-nication and information technology; aviation; rotations; capacity building; property management; rations; fuel; water; and vehicles and other equipment. These support areas are financed through the assessed contributions of mem-ber states. Since the authorisation by the UNSC, therefore, funding has been made available to UNSOA to facilitate provision of these services. To date, $729 million has been disbursed from the assessed budget to UNSOA to im-plement the AMISOM logistical support package.

However, other critical requirements of AMISOM are not catered for and financed through assessed contributions of member states. It is in this context that Resolution 1863 also requested the UN Secretary-General 'to establish a trust fund to provide financial support to AMISOM until a United Nations Peacekeeping Operation is deployed'. This UN trust fund, to which member states have been encouraged to make donations on several occasions, is the funding stream aimed at supporting AMISOM in areas not covered by assessed funding but critical to its mandate and to ensuring that AMISOM is brought up to UN standards.

Thus, certain critical mission support areas do not have guaranteed, sustainable and predictable funding but depend on the whims and caprices of member states. The support areas financed through the AMISOM trust fund include reimbursement for contingent-owned equipment, medical support, civilian and police operational costs, including safety and security equipment, and travel and administration costs.

Despite the good intentions behind the trust fund, which has received about $43 million to date, it remains a purse for voluntary contributions made on the basis of the goodwill and, if I may add, the interests of contributing member states. Its voluntary nature leaves it with several limitations. Since its establishment, a major limitation has been the caveats placed with regard, in particular, to offsetting military expenditures, especially those of a lethal nature.

On the whole, UNSOA has done a commendable job in setting up the logistical support package, but there have been some related communication, coordination and delivery challenges. The communication and coordination challenges, I would say, are teething problems related to the unprecedented nature of the AMISOM-UNSOA marriage, but the delivery aspects may not be unrelated to the level of expectations of AMISOM. I highlight a few of the challenges below.

As regards communication and coordination, the memorandum of understanding between the AU and UN identifies the Special Representative for Somalia (SRCC)/Head of Mission (HoM) as the AU coordinator and the UNSOA director as UN coordinator. However, there have been instances when communication and coordination between AMISOM and UNSOA did not originate with official coordinators, thus creating problems that would otherwise have been avoided. This was commonplace in the period when there was no civilian management (in particular, the chief administrative officer of AMISOM) in the mission area, leaving UNSOA with no choice but to engage force headquarters directly. A further complication has been UNSOA's occasional direct engagement with TCCs without the necessary involvement of AUPSOD or AMISOM.

In terms of substantive support expectations, a major and persistent deficit relates to the need to extend logistical support to the civilian component of AMISOM. This has been discussed at length and my conclusion is that this omission stems from a divergence in interpretation between the AU and UN of Resolution 1863 and the UN Secretary-General's letters and their annexes S/2008/804 and S/2009/60 to the UNSC dated 19 December 2008 and 30 January 2009 respectively. Structurally, such issues as gaps in civilian staffing in AMISOM and differences between the AU and UN budget and planning cycles also impact the delivery of the substantial support elements, sometimes straining the relationship on the ground.

Other funding and support mechanisms, including EU support to the AU and bilateral contributions to TCCs

The third pillar of support to AMISOM comes in two forms. One involves financial support to the AU for the planning, deployment and management of AMISOM. As noted earlier, these costs have since 2007 been borne by the European Commission (EC) to the tune of €258/$347 million. Some EU member states have also been providing bilateral support to the AU to cover certain operational costs and projects implemented in support of the Somali population. The EC financial support has been used to cover troop and police allowances. The second channel of support goes directly, through bilateral arrangements, to countries contributing troops to AMISOM. In this case, the US stands out for providing pre-deployment training and force protection equipment to both Burundi and Uganda.

Recommendations and Way Forward

Obviously, when aggregated, the various financing and support mechanisms for AMISOM amount to a significant package. Indeed, it is significant that the UNSC has even mandated the provision of logistical support to AMISOM. In itself, this is recognition of the need for, as the UN Secretary-General aptly explained in his exchange of letters to the UNSC, a joint effort between the UN Secretariat and member states to support AMISOM. However, two questions arise. One, which I have referred to earlier, is why do we have such a complex support scenario for AMISOM? And secondly: Is the support sufficient to facilitate the effective implementation of the AMISOM mandate?

Clearly, the logistical support package delivered by UNSOA has contributed significantly to AMISOM's successes. There have been marked improvements in sustenance, camp security, accommodation, food, and so on. However, there are the deficiencies I discussed earlier. In my view, UNSOA is an implementing agency delivering only on what it has been mandated to deliver. The problem lies with the mandating authority that sets out the policy directives and the Secretariat, which outlines the operational guidelines.

The AU and UN, which have a common objective to restore peace and security in Somalia and agree that AMISOM is in Somalia on behalf of the international community, should concur on the imperative need to adequately support and equip AMISOM to deliver on its mandate. AMISOM has been deployed in Somalia for five years now, a feat not matched by any other mission. It has made significant gains, but these have come at a very high human cost when we consider the death and disability statistics of the mission. Could we have prevented or at least reduced these costs?

In view of the above, I would like to submit the following recommendations:

At the Policy Level

• There is the need for enhanced engagement between the UN Secretariat and AU Commission, on one hand, and the UNSC and AUPSC on the other especially for purposes of shared/joint analysis. Beyond transmission of decisions, there is a need for prior discussion regarding the rationale for them in order to measure the appetite of the UNSC to endorse and authorise the required support for the implementation of such decisions.

At the Planning Level

• The UN planning team has been in post for three years now and has provided significant support to the AU with regard to the planning, deployment and management of AMISOM. However, a number of gaps need to be addressed to make this assistance more effective. For our part, the AU also needs to have a fullyfledged planning team. This can be achieved by enhancing the structure of the peace and security department and AUPSOD. The lesson here is that where there are no AU counterparts, we have witnessed capacity substitution rather than capacity building. For its part, the UN needs to be cognizant of certain contextual peculiarities and personality idiosyncrasies in posting personnel to the AU. Capacity building through staff exchanges between the AU and UN can also be useful.

At the Support Level

- There are some challenges with the implementation of the UN-AU memorandum of understanding on support delivery by UNSOA. Two years into its implementation, there is a need to review and, where necessary, revise the memorandum based on lessons learnt thus far. We would need to take heed of the fact that AMISOM is not a typical peacekeeping operation: the principles for a UN peacekeeping operation do not exist in Somalia because a war is going on, yet AMISOM is deployed on the ground. There is therefore the need for flexibility in the delivery of the support package.

While support to uniformed AMISOM personnel is working relatively well, the exclusion of AMISOM's civilian component from the logistical support package needs to be addressed. If the intention is to build the capacity of the AU to plan, deploy and manage its missions, a responsibility which the AU entrusts to the civilian component of its missions, it is necessary for this gap to be closed. The spirit and letter of Resolution 1863 need to be respected in both their interpretation and implementation.

Conclusion

Somalia presents some very peculiar challenges that both the AU and UN should appreciate. The reality is that we are charting new waters with the UN utilising UN resources to support what could be referred to as an external client (AU) in practically a war situation. What this requires is plenty of understanding of the situation and mutual understanding of our respective institutional appetites, capacities and cultures in relation to the situation. Do we have to go outside the rules on occasion, especially when practically so required? I believe we cannot afford to do things in the way we are used to, neither as the AU with our limited experience nor as the UN drawing on 60 years of peacekeeping experience. Ultimately, what is required is a comprehensive package that guarantees resourcing to the AU in a predictable and sustainable manner so that it has sufficient capacity to meet the challenges of peacekeeping or peace support on the continent, because, clearly, all indications point to that need.

In conclusion, AMISOM requires a guaranteed and predictable funding mechanism and this can only be assured through the UN-assessed budget. I am aware that the appetite for re-hatting AMISOM is lacking, most especially given the assumption it will be much more costly, and that UN peacekeeping in Somalia is not exactly a palatable option. The way forward may be to retain AMISOM as is, reinforcing it and providing it with UN-assessed funding.

7. Challenges, Key Issues and Future Directions

Linnéa Gelot, Ludwig Gelot and Cedric de Coning

Introduction

Over the last decades, various models of AU-UN collaboration have been implemented with varying degrees of success. All stakeholders have faced numerous challenges and obstacles at all levels. Far from being solely financial, major issues also arose at the political, operational and technical levels. As one seminar participant stated, the 'challenges of peacekeeping go far beyond funding issues. Lessons learned from previous African-led missions are important.'

Therefore, this part of the report identifies the various obstacles faced by the stakeholders in the cases of AMIS, UNAMID and AMISOM. In the first section, we consider a series of cross-cutting issues that have affected stakeholder relations in all three missions. In particular, we consider issues of strategic thinking, funding and AU-UN synergy. This short assessment of relations between AU, UN, donors and host states is followed by discussions of the four case studies: AMIS; UNAMID; peace operations and joint mediation; and AMISOM. Seminar participants have written detailed assessments regarding the implementation of 'jointness', hybridity and support models in their respective areas of expertise.

Stakeholder Relations and Strategic Thinking

The key stakeholders in the AU-UN support models debate are the Secretariats, the key donors of APSA, the African RECs and all the AU and UN state members. The seminar emphasised that the AU and the UN need to invest more in the relationship, as do all stakeholders. As one participant explained 'Thus far, little strategic thinking has gone into the cooperation.' Another participant added, 'The understanding of challenges is looked at differently from New York, Brussels and Addis Ababa.' In turn, this lack of shared strategic vision has had important implications for the mandates of peace operations jointly led by AU and UN as well as for missions led by the AU but supported by the UN and/or donors. Stakeholders have implemented different interpretations of international peace and security thereby affecting the overall effectiveness of missions. But the lack of strategic agreement has also had adverse implications for international consensus, sustainable funding, effective synergy and adequate peacekeeping standards.

In the case of Sudan, the lack of strategic agreement has rendered international consensus too elusive to create political conditions propitious for the success of operations. Indeed, the lack of consensus in regard to the Darfur conflict has made it easier for the government of Sudan to manipulate and withdraw its consent on critical aspects of the peace operations on its territory. When international consensus on how to address a conflict is weak or nonexistent, a host state can exploit the gaps in policies to further divide the players involved and to ensure slow or ineffective action. While strategic discussions will not unify the views and positions of the stakeholders on the most effective approach to a specific conflict, greater institutionalisation (such as coming with prepared positions to joint meetings, sending the best people to consultations, exchanges, training sessions, etc.) would help smooth AU-UN consultations and high-level meetings. In turn, this would facilitate the emergence of a shared understanding of the situation and possibly a more united front in tackling conflicts on the African continent.

Besides international consensus, the lack of strategic agreement has also affected the securing of a sustainable and relatively predictable source of funding for peace operations. All seminar participants agreed that the AU needs long-term and sustainable funding as well as capacity building. This would not only facilitate operations but would also strengthen stakeholder relations. In this context, the AU demand for some sort of automatic funding from the UN is unlikely to be answered affirmatively and some sort of middle way must be found to avoid the current gaps in funding. Seminar participants were candid on this issue and explained that the conversation of recent years will not progress since 'the UNSC will not decide on automaticity for AUPSC decisions'. Indeed, UNSC members fear that such a decision would lessen their political control. But besides funding from the UN, the AU must also face current challenges in the context of uprisings in North Africa. The existing yet insufficient AU funding mechanisms are faced with great uncertainties as a result of the Arab Spring, as noted by one seminar participant:

> Will the AU as a political project be viable, with funding no longer there from North African countries (Libya and Egypt – the operating budget of AU)? What about the recession and the Euro crisis? When discussing hybridity we need to think about the financial limits faced by the AU after the Arab Spring.

There is a widespread agreement that funding models should be appropriate, timely and more predictable. While this is clearly not a remedy for all the problems arising from AU-UN collaboration, it will facilitate joint action. Specific issues that require further discussion include the proposal that AU headquarters could standardise internal audits of PSOs [authors: spell out] from the beginning to the end, as well as the proposal that a board of directors manage the Peace Fund to increase its transparency and effectiveness. Steps such as these might encourage member states and Western countries to increase their contributions. Also, as one participant put it, 'if the AU member states do not invest long-term in the AU's peace and security role, how can they ask donors to continue the funding?'

This lack of stable strategic agreement at the continental and international levels places a strain on relations that, as contributions to this report have shown, have already adversely affected operations on the ground. Participants agree that there is a need to further discuss the comparative advantages to all stakeholders of increased synergy and capacity building. What are the comparative advantages of the AU and how can one leverage them? First of all this would avoid duplication of roles and it could harmonise the relationship between the AU, members states and the RECs. Second, it would be easier for AU staff to formulate needs to the UN and other partners. And third, it would be easier for the AU and partners to know what they are preparing and training peace operation staff for (what types of skills, tasks, missions). If comparative advantages could be clarified and better understood, this could enable capacity-building projects to be based on a principle of complementary rather than capacity-substitution, as it is too often the case now. AU member states must be directly engaged in this discussion in order to ascertain their vision of the role of the AU in peace and security on the continent. This would cover issues of non-compliance and assessed contributions of AU member states as well as the ability of the host state to withdraw/manipulate consent. Indeed, this is not a technical issue since it springs from AU principles and organisational structure.

Finally, the lack of strategic agreement is also being felt in regard to peacekeeping standards. During the seminar, this issue led to intense debate. On one hand, the AU might have certain comparative advantages such as the speed with which troops can be deployed and the willingness to deploy to volatile and insecure areas. On the other, some military units deployed on AU missions may at times have lacked the training, preparedness and capability expected of UN contributors. In AMISOM, for instance, some troops were deployed with insufficient training and without critical equipment for the tasks expected of them. In this regard, one participant said, 'We talk about international standards of peacekeeping but the reality is different.'

Another participant argued that this lack of common or minimum standards can at times also be a positive attribute. For instance, when the mission leadership has to use troops optimally and when those troops are not overly cautious or concerned about all kinds of minimum standards, they can sometimes be used more flexibly than in UN peace operations, where units sometimes use minimum standards as a reason not to be deployed into more dangerous or uncomfortable locations. It was suggested that UN standards go too far in terms of welfare and troop protection, and that they could be reviewed and made more flexible.

The perceived difference between UN standards and AU practice can, however, contribute to a culture in which stakeholders and AU partners come to expect African actors to conduct peace operations 'on the cheap'. In the support models debate, this could result in partners supporting AU missions at minimum levels, that is, enough support to have peacekeepers on the ground, but not enough to enable them to achieve their mission.

One participant exclaimed, 'There is no such thing as African standards of peacekeeping.' Many participants agreed that African troops should be afforded the same training and equipment as other troops in UN and multilateral peace operations. But others disagreed, describing UN standards as too high. One participant used the example of the culinary needs of African troops from a specific nation to make the point that there always has to be accommodation between general standards and specific cultural practices. Some participants observed that when the UN supports African missions, UN standards can become obstacles that undermine progress and efficiency in the field, especially in warlike situations such as Somalia. In the case of AMISOM, there seems to have been a gap between the level of support the AU needed for its high intensity operations, for instance, the munitions expended and the number of wounded soldiers needing medical treatment, and the standard for UN peacekeeping operations, where munitions are rarely used and the number of peacekeepers needing medical care is much lower.

The above issues are broadly representative of the adverse implications of the lack of strategic agreement among the AU, UN and other stakeholders. They affect peace operations and should be seen as an incentive to further institutionalise collaboration. It is necessary to work on the strategic relationship between the UNSC and AUPSC since there is 'no doubt that AU-UN collaboration must continue and must be deepened'.

Having outlined the key cross-cutting issues in stakeholder relations, we turn to the specific challenges faced by existing support models. The thread running through all the experiences to date is the sense that the models have not come about as a result of long-term strategic thinking. Rather, they developed organically in response to what was politically expedient and as a constant process of working around obstacles. However, participants also acknowledged that planning has its dangers, since pre-designed fixed models can become straitjackets when flexibility is most needed. Instead, it seems that what must be strengthened is the quality of the relationship between partners, the establishment of effective communication channels and shared strategic thinking.

Direct Donor Support Model (AMIS)

AMIS (2004–07) began as a military observer mission. In October 2004, AMIS grew into a larger peace operation comprising approximately 2,200 personnel, including force protectors and unarmed civilian police. The AU-led peace operation had the strategic consent of the government in Khartoum, but all the operational actions of the mission had to be negotiated over and over again to maintain that consent. The AU also had to balance global humanitarian appeals, the divergent views of the AU membership and the priorities of foreign donors. Amid rampant violations by all parties, the AU upgraded AMIS's mandate and increased its force levels. AMIS's new tasks were to monitor the situation proactively and report any violations to the relevant organs; assist in the process of confidence-building; and to contribute to a secure environment for the delivery of humanitarian relief.

AMIS was also tasked with 'protect[ing] civilians whom it encounters under imminent threat and in the immediate vicinity, within resources and capability, it being understood that the protection of the civilian population is the responsibility of the government of Sudan' (AU 2004:65–7). This was the first time an AU peace operation was explicitly mandated to protect civilians. The UNSC endorsed the enhanced mandate (UNSC 2004).

By December 2005, AMIS had almost 7,000 personnel on the ground and a stronger civilian police component of about 1,320. This increase in numbers helped stabilise the security situation in the region. During 2005 and 2006, AMIS carried out some innovative – yet selective and *ad hoc* – civilian protection measures, such as water and firewood patrols and on market days. The AUPSC and AUPSOD provided the mission leadership with very little strategic guidance or directives concerning its key tasks. In practice, the priority was monitoring the humanitarian ceasefire agreement. AMIS did not engage armed groups when they attacked civilians. All along, the Khartoum government ignored the AUPC's condemnations and 'appeals' for it to disarm the Janjaweed. The unwillingness to challenge the sovereignty of the government of Sudan, whose consent was required for the mission to be able to carry out its work, characterised not just the AU but all the international actors involved in supporting AMIS.

The UN Secretariat advised and assisted the AU with human resources (military and police advisers and civilians), training, skills and limited logistics. Donor support was important. The mobility of AMIS was highly dependent on the vehicles, civilian helicopters and fixed-wing aircraft provided by its partners. However, such support was piecemeal, short-term and unreliable. AMIS operated at a standard far below what is normal in UN peace operations. For instance, partners did not follow through on a March 2005 recommendation to provide AMIS with attack helicopters, the lack of which in the subsectors of Darfur was a substantial hindrance. Civilian pilots could not be ordered to fly in dangerous circumstances, so helicopters could not be used to avert attacks on civilian populations. The civilian helicopters had to be back in El Fasher before 6 pm owing to the 6 pm to 6 am curfew that the government of Sudan imposed on AMIS in 2005.

The signing of the Darfur peace agreement on 5 May 2006 was the culmination of the AU-led mediation. Only the government of Sudan and the Minni Minawi faction of the SLM signed, while JEM and the Abdel Wahid al Nur faction of the SLM rejected the agreement. The process was rushed and abruptly ended by the British and US envoys, who grew tired of funding the talks. Soon after, more elements of Darfuri society began to perceive AMIS as siding with the host state. The Darfur rebellion fractured into more than 15 groups. The US, Canada and the EU were keen to stop funding the AU force. They argued for a UN takeover, since there was formally a peace agreement in place. A UN takeover would shift the financial responsibility to the UN in place of continuing donor money. Significant pressure was placed on the government of Sudan, which still objected to a UN takeover. On 31 August 2006, the UNSC adopted Resolution 1706 'inviting' Khartoum to consent to a UN takeover. AU-UN joint political and technical assessment missions were deployed to Sudan and Darfur to persuade al-Bashir to allow in a Chapter VII UN force. Khartoum still did not consent. The intensified AU-UN collaboration and a mood of compromise in the international community were key factors for the agreement by the US and China to a compromise proposal by Kofi Annan on 16 November 2006. The five permanent members of the UNSC, the AUPSC members, a number of African countries, the government of Sudan, the EU and the Arab League agreed to the 'hybrid' UN-AU force proposal at a high-level meeting co-chaired by the UN Secretary-General and the AU Commission chairperson.

The agreement indicated that the mission should have a predominantly 'African character' and troops should, as far as possible, be sourced from African countries. The transition would occur in three phases, with UN-funded light and heavy support packages before the actual takeover. This allowed the UN to boost AMIS and simultaneously build up its presence in steps, without provoking the Sudanese regime. Sudan eventually consented in June 2007. On 31 July 2007, the UNSC unanimously adopted Resolution 1769, which authorised UNAMID under Chapter VII of the UN Charter to implement the Darfur peace agreement and to protect both civilians and its own personnel.

'Ad-hocery'

Seminar participants pointed to several challenges with direct donor support models. In the case of AMIS, most agreed the mission led to insufficient capacity building because the support mechanisms and structures were *ad hoc* and reactive, and were not designed to be made permanent. Anyidoho in his paper calls the support disjointed. Too little technical know-how and knowledge stayed with the AU afterwards. By that time, the AU did not have many civilian and military staff, and partners had to provide experts for the Darfur Integrated Task Force. But this was a one-mission office and the capacity built over this time was not harnessed in a strategic way by AUPSOD or the AU Commission. In terms of ownership, the AU remained dependent and reliant on the complex web of interested, disjointed donors, and had no option but to accept the conditionalities. The force commander could not instruct a donor-contracted helicopter to evacuate people because the contractors were civilians. Civilian pilots cannot be ordered to carry out high-risk tasks. This problem is not unique to AMIS, as normal UN peace operations face the same constraints when utilising civilian-contracted helicopter services. However, what made the situation even more difficult in the AMIS context was that the contracts were not between AMIS and the service providers, but between a specific donor and a service provider. This necessitated complicated negotiations when the tasks performed by service providers needed to be adapted to changing circumstances.

Camp facilities were a particular problem. One participant remarked that the 'accommodation was in bad shape: had they not been African troops they would have mutinied'. Some participants were more positive about the lessons learned during AMIS: 'There has been a lot of consolidation of learning by the AU after this operation.' The progress is seen in how direct donor support works better today in the AMISOM mission. Support is accounted for in better ways, the AU finance department is bigger and its auditing and management is of higher quality. In AMISOM, external auditors come back from the field and have nothing to report. The EU has not had to recover any funds for lack of auditing. However, while the finance department might have grown and improved, there was still the concern that, 'lessons learned are really pockets of learning and not systematic or long-term capacity building.' Especially in AUPSOD there is a need to increase capability, human as well as material. The unit needs more political direction, greater ability to plan ahead and more independence from donor interests.

Start-up phase vs bridging mission

Direct donor support models work best when the urgency of the situation requires quick action, before normal political decision-making has had time to run its course. That makes such models more suitable by nature for small-scale, time-limited operations and in the early stages of missions. While direct donor support allows both the AU and partners to make a start before the UNSC has decided to transform the AU mission into a UN mission, it can just as easily be a negative if it contributes to UNSC's postponement of taking over the mission on the grounds that a 'good enough' mission is already on the ground. With reference to 'African solutions', the UNSC might justify international inaction for a long time, until the mission donors put enough pressure on the UN or withdraw their funding for the African mission. If donors do this when no other funding is in place, the mission is left in a difficult tactical position (as was the situation for AMIS in 2006).

One tool in the toolbox

Even if there were problems with direct donor support to AMIS, a few participants said that the model should still be considered as one tool in the toolbox. Just as AMIS was a pilot project for the AU, the direct support to AMIS was also a first for donors, such as the EU. The specific challenges involved in the AMIS mission should not be equated with problems with the model. Some of those challenges arose from the AU's decision to launch AMIS without the ability to fund, plan, recruit for or manage the mission. Others had to do with the EU and other donors, who had to work out in real time what to support the AU with and how to ensure accountability. Around 20 donors provided funding for the start-up of the operation. Coordination between these donors and with the AU was a challenge – the AU being understaffed and each of the donors coming with its own instructions on how to spend the money and report on it. The EU spent more than €300 million on this operation alone. EU funding was as flexible as possible but was drawn from a development fund and could not finance weapons. Some partners preferred to give support in kind rather than financial support. This complicated the AU's task of allocating and efficiently managing the different streams of support. As one participant noted, 'Given all these challenges … AMIS was reasonably successful.'

To sum up, direct donor support is one model in the toolbox and appropriate for small-scale operations or for the early stages of an operation, when the UN is unable to provide support or before it takes over a mission. However, funding disruptions can jeopardise the peacekeepers' tactical legitimacy. Funding needs to be better harmonised. The AUPSC needs to give clearer instructions on what type of mission it deploys. AMIS started out as a military observer mission, but over time became a peace operation with a broad mandate, including protection of the civilian population of Darfur. The AUPSC and TCCs are directly responsible for the mission's mandate and activities in the field, and so are UNSC members and other stakeholders.

Hybrid AU-UN Mediation Model

Shared agenda

The seminar recognised that the AU-UN joint mediation process was challenging for both organisations, largely due to their different interpretations of conflict situations in Africa. This meant that AU-UN mediators and their staff at times worked with different approaches and priorities to secure peace in Darfur. Banseka's reflections on AU-UN joint mediation conclude that although the UN brings with it the requisite finances for political talks, the organisational culture – the UN's *modus operandi* – constrains the emergence of a genuine partnership. The UNSC approach has sometimes led to negative perceptions on the part of the AU as well as some African leaders and parties to conflicts. Too often the UNSC is seen as dictating Western priorities and treating the AU as less capable, knowledgeable and professional. This fragmentation made it easier for individual states with an interest in the Darfur issue to appoint envoys to try to influence and direct the process. A few participants criticised the AU for pursuing its own approach and for its inability to stand up to a strong AU member state. A mediation initiative took place in Sirte, Libya, where Gadaffi's involvement was not constructive. The AU, already seen as a state-biased mediator by being too soft on the Sudan government, lost further credibility. The lack of shared agenda rendered joint mediation imprecise and ambiguous. This weakness became more apparent, as Banseka explains in his chapter, after the AU later created an AU high-level panel on Darfur. This panel was to articulate the AU vision, thereby raising the question of why the AU would not articulate this through the policy mechanism already in place, the joint Salim-Eliasson and the later Bassolé initiatives. One participant explained that the 'AU and UN decided that it would be better to have one mediator, resident in Sudan. But some in the AU complained that Bassolé was West-leaning and reported only to the UNSC. But the cables were sent to both the UNSC and the AUPSC.' The tensions culminated over the International Criminal Court indictment of Al-Bashir, an issue supported on the UN side and vehemently opposed on the AU side.

Mutual legitimacy

Joint AU-UN mediation recognises that African wars are not just an African affair. As Banseka's chapter explains, bringing in the UN as joint mediator was meant to mirror the international community's concerns about the Darfur crisis. Joint mediation can strengthen legitimacy of the participating organisations. In the Darfur case, the UN lent political support to the AU so that the AU could stay as a lead mediator at a time when rebel factions saw it as deeply biased in favour of the government of Sudan. In a partnership, reciprocal political support is especially important where a strong host state such as Sudan is very distrustful and obstructs or breaches agreements and UNSC resolutions. Joint mediation in Darfur was perhaps a decidedly 'hard case', but the AU-UN partnership would do well to be prepared for similar cases in the future. It is telling that, according to one person, 'the neutrality of the mediators became a major issue. The UN had to spend the first 6 months of the mediation convincing the parties to accept the AU's role. The AU was seen as pushing Bashir's agenda, many Darfuris felt (after the experience with the Abuja/Darfur peace agreement process).' The AU and the UN should reassess how to better support one another. Such support needs to be genuine and not simply a façade.

Organisational cultures

Banseka states that the AU approach to conflict resolution tends to be more ethnocentric, while the UN has longstanding bureaucratic and 'universal' mechanisms for resolving differences. The AU promotes the fostering of shared African values, and criticises 'undue interventionism' by the West in African politics. Just as frequent is the rhetoric that the AU needs to work with, invite and learn from the UN's wealth of experience (desirable multilateralism). The AU position, namely that the conflict in Darfur was an African conflict requiring an African solution, impacted the organisation's *modus operandi*. Banseka shows us that the AU regarded both Eliasson and Bassolé as 'Western' and 'foreign', leading to frictions in the mediation team. For their part, the UN partners insinuated (in private) that the only interest AU authorities had in the mediation was nepotism. The political reality of the Darfur mediation was partly that, as one person said, 'the AU does not have in-depth experience of mediation.'

The AU is a multilateral organisation but lacks international weight since it lacks its own financial support structure and is not financially independent. This was evident when the Darfur peace agreement came to a premature close after the bilateral donors (UK, US) stopped their funding flows. The joint mediation model held out the promise of easing funding issues. Even so, despite access to a multimillion dollar trust fund, the mediation was dependent on UNAMID for its financial and administrative operations and delays and other problems were numerous.

Participants nonetheless held that there may be further opportunities for joint AU-UN mediation. In future cases, common strategic decisions at a political level are needed early on to bridge the different approaches favoured by the UNSC and the AUPSC and the divide between the conflicting parties. Often in Darfur, only 'lowest common denominator' decisions could be made. Another perspective in the group was that the 'jointness of approach' notion undermined both partners, at least in the case of Darfur (as in the Salim-Eliasson mediation track). Striving for jointness is too ambitious, and 'parallel partnership' seems more realistic (for example, the Haile Menkarios-Thabo Mbeki high level panel as it applied to the implementation of the Sudan-South Sudan comprehensive peace agreement). While jointness might work in some cases, the political context can change quickly and can result in tension as both organisations respond differently. In the Darfur process, the International Criminal Court indictment of Al-Bashir was an instance of how political context can rapidly change the stakes and potential for the AU and UN. Related to this, one participant held that a model requiring high levels of harmonisation and cooperation (such as the envisaged genuine joint and hybrid peace operations) may not be suitable in volatile situations, such as ongoing wars.

Summing up, the AU-UN partnership has to be understood against the backdrop of an asymmetrical power relationship. The UNSC has the authority to define what counts as a threat to international peace and security and the big powers can use their privileged memberships in this body to pursue what they view as best for them and what they feel is right. These policies and decisions sometimes run counter to the dominant AU perspective on what approach would ensure peace in a given African crisis. Partnership between the AU and UN under these circumstances will always have to strike a fine balance between national interests and multilateralism. The AU is acutely aware of its lesser power in this relationship and, among other things, continues to push for an African seat on the UNSC. When it comes to joint mediation processes, the mediators need to spend considerable time in building confidence among all stakeholders in the region. A single AU-UN mediator may work better than two. The local politics will always impact and sometimes undermine joint AU-UN mediation ventures.

Hybrid AU-UN Mission Model (UNAMID)

UNAMID is the UN's first hybrid mission with the AU, and it became operational on 31 December 2007. It is funded through the UN assessed contributions budget. UNAMID was authorised at force levels of 26,000 personnel, and a US$1.48 Billion budget was approved for the first year. This was the UN's biggest ever approved estimate for a single peace operation (UNGA 2007). UNAMID led to intense debate about political control, leadership and access to UN resources. One sticking point was whether the operation should be viewed as a true example of, or as an attempt at hybridity.

When AMIS was transformed into UNAMID, the 'Annan package' was that the hybridity would become a reality in three steps: the light support package, the heavy support package and finally the full hybrid mission. Participants debated whether UNSC members and donors, as well as the host state, implemented this consensus package to the letter. UNAMID began operations with little of the logistical and lethal equipment (critical parts of the heavy support package) that it needed to implement its mandate. Thus, Anyidoho's chapter wonders: was it hybridity, or direct donor support by another name? The group discussed the weaknesses to date of support models that include military components, especially when military equipment does not materialise quickly or in sufficient amounts. The mission was constrained by its limited mobility, inadequate logistical capacity, poor radio access and weak command-and-control. Only Ethiopia sent acceptable tactical helicopters, numbering five in 2010. The build-up of the mission was slow. In July 2008, after six months on the ground, UNAMID comprised only 9,400 troops, mostly ex-AMIS forces. By 30 November 2008, the total strength of UNAMID had reached 15,444. By 31 October 2010, UNAMID's total strength was 21,797. As of 30 June 2011, UNAMID's total personnel strength was 25,231. As one participant explained, 'African countries that offered to provide troops and police were still waiting for donor support from outside. In the first year we had only one formed police unit from Bangladesh instead of 17.'

Another participant was even more critical, 'Was this because countries do this for visibility back home, more so than to help AU peacekeeping? Or did they forget what they had agreed to in these packages?' The feeling was that this undermined the hybrid mission significantly: since UNAMID began operations with such little visible difference between AMIS standards and its own standards, the people of Darfur immediately lost hope that this hybrid mission could bring peace, protection or stability. Agwai's chapter stresses the national interest factor and suggests that the AUPSC and UNSC need to work closely, and,

> ... if need be, to lobby neutral countries such as Sweden, other Nordic countries, other regional organisations and powers to push the permanent UNSC members to be more even-handed in mandating peacekeeping missions in Africa or to help provide resources for the AU to effectively undertake missions, for example in Somalia. Having the support of 'sponsors' such as the US, UK, France, Russia and China in their historical spheres of influence is a critical factor

Good leadership

It was held that a senior joint head of mission has the challenging task of bringing the organisations closer together, and of mediating among the AU-UN and the host state. Joint Special Representative Ibrahim Gambari was considered to have done this well, given the challenging circumstances. UNAMID's primary mission objective is civilian protection and in strategic documents this role has been clearly formulated and described. However, initially there was no strategy to prepare and empower the UNAMID leadership or its troops for this task in a comprehensive way. Practically, UNAMID 'engages and assists' the government of Sudan in carrying out its primary responsibilities for protecting civilians in Darfur in accordance with international obligations. Above all, Ibrahim Gambari and his office have been negotiating with the national authorities in carrying out their protection responsibilities and to follow up at relevant levels in those numerous instances when access is denied and the Status of Forces Agreement is breached.

UNAMID's leaders have argued all along that implementing the mandate was very difficult in a situation of ongoing hostilities and in the absence of a comprehensive peace deal between Khartoum and the rebels. Both the UNSC and AUPSC were unwilling to directly enforce decisions on the government of Sudan, sovereignty and international order weighing heavier than specific human rights concerns. This can be seen in what the mandate (UNSC Resolution 1769) did not include, such as detailing robust sanctions against Khartoum in cases of non-compliance and the authorisation of UNAMID to collect arms. Moreover, Anyidoho's chapter recounts that at the time of the indictment of Al-Bashir in July 2008, UNAMID at one point had to relocate some of its staff and the security phase of the mission was raised. Even then the mission had to continue to deal with the indicted president in order to implement its mandate.

Knowledge transfer/capacity building

In UNAMID, many senior officials have gained important experience from working side by side. Some knowledge transfer resulted from this proximity. One participant felt that hybrid models are a good idea, but 'to improve peacekeeping in Africa what is needed is technical know-how and knowledge.' Another critically remarked:

> If donors wanted to help the AU with peacekeeping in Africa why not contribute genuine and useful support? Why bring old, used things for which there are no spare parts? Why contract the Pacific Architects and Engineers to do food, and tell us that even the FC [force commander] has no mandate to ask about what troops eat. Why bring communication equipment where one still has to ring London for support?

Shared ownership by both partners

Hybrids might increase a mutual sense of ownership, but drawing on the case of UNAMID several participants stressed that the AUPSC would need to show more involvement in future hybrid missions. This includes communicating more with mission leadership and giving more visibility and support to the mission. Even though it was agreed that UNAMID would follow UN command and control procedures, the mission's leadership often felt that AUPSC and AU member states should stay more involved.

We felt closer to UN headquarters in New York. The UN provided modern communications systems and visited regularly. Addis was silent. It was hard to follow directions from two HQs when it took so much time and Addis was not up to speed. We had to take bold decisions and bear consequences or people would die.

One critical perspective of the AUHQ was that it did not want to visit or spend time in Darfur. In the UNAMID case, the AU is not supposed to respond to all cables coming in on a day to day basis. Strategic political guidance should come from UN and AU with one voice. Anyidoho also counters that it was unclear what was meant by UNAMID's operating under UN rules and regulations. For the UN, once the mission was to be financially supported from UN assessed contributions, everything was to be done according to established procedures. But what sense of ownership would this leave the AU?

For the hybrid model to work better, AU member states would need to be more united behind the AU peace and security role. 'For the AU, peacekeeping is a flagship enterprise. The AUPSC needs to be more active and serious.' This includes what people the AU employs and how it attempts to keep good staff within the organisation. During the course of UNAMID's operations, 'too many AU officers became UN officers and will not come back except as well paid consultants.'

AU-UN comparative advantage

The viability of hybrids depends in part on how well they are constructed. As the Abdallah and Aning chapter argues, hybrids may bring together several advantages: the AU harnesses troops to intervene in situations where arguably there is no peace to keep, responds as a stabilisation force, reduces civilian casualties and maintains relative peace and security with funds and logistics provided by the UN. For its part, the UN has a demonstrated capacity to sustain long-term multidimensional missions. Hybrid missions need to place a responsibility to finance and provide logistics on the developed and Western states. One advantage with hybrids is that the UN's involvement helps secure more troop contributions, also from TCCs outside Africa. Many African states are reluctant to accept postings under AU-sponsored missions because the organisation lacks the financial capacity to meet its commitments and to supply the logistics and equipment needed to ensure the safety and security of peacekeepers.

Abdallah and Aning make a cautious argument for developing the hybrid model, on condition the AU-UN partnership is further formalised. Another condition is that future mandates for hybrid missions must be comprehensive and reflect the size of the peacekeeping force and the broader security challenges in the mission state (not setting the mission up to fail). Mandates should be realistic, not using language which promises physical protection when the UNSC and AUPSC in reality lack the appetite to challenge the sovereignty of the host state. A third is that the UN and other bilateral donor agencies should coordinate their efforts in developing a much stronger APSA and the operationalisation of its pillars, particularly the ASF.

To these conditions, Banseka's chapter adds the quality of relationships. Hybrid operations 'will only work if both organisations wield considerable political and financial power, and have the same vision and *modus operandi*, and if they are able to deal with one another in an equitable, open and respectful way'. He continues:

> As long as there are competing ideologies and each seeks to push its own agenda and insist that its vision should prevail; as long as there is not enough flexibility on the part of both organisations; and as long as the AU does not have the money and human resources for self-help, the hybrid concept and contemporary support models might come to have more ingredients for failure than success.

Anyidoho emphasises the need of the AU to clarify its strategic approach and its political initiatives. He adds that in a hybrid model in a Darfur-like scenario, the mission needs to have a humanitarian mandate. UNAMID had to support one of the world's largest humanitarian operations without the requisite mandate. Agwai's chapter also notes that hybrids are only successful if national, regional and international powers work together.

Staff Training, Capacity Building

Anyidoho proposes that in future hybrids it is important that absorbing AU staff into AU-UN missions leads to AU capacity building. Qualified AMIS staff were taken on board as UN staff, since this was financially rewarding to the individuals. Instead, the AU could second some of its current staff to UNAMID on a rotational basis for six months. The placements should be in both substantive sections and mission support. Officials would then learn how the UN operates: financial regulations and compliance, recruitment processes, logistical support and supply chain management, coordination with humanitarian organisations, political reporting, accountability, etc. Anyidoho concludes that the AMIS/UNAMID models, which were born of necessity, have reduced violence and saved many lives.

UN Assessed Contribution Model (AMISOM)

The AMISOM section of the seminar focused on challenges arising from having several support models at play simultaneously and from unclear concepts of operations, especially in a highly volatile and complex warlike context. The support to AMISOM included a trust fund, the use of the EU African Peace Fund for troop allowances and equipment, direct donor support (key donors include UK, Spain, Germany, Italy, Turkey, China), and UNSOA, which runs on the UN assessed contributions budget. The panel primarily evaluated the UNSOA-AMISOM relationship.

UN and flexibility

The UN Secretariat has gone to unprecedented lengths to provide support flexibly through UNSOA. For example, UNSC Resolution 1863 broke new ground, since it allowed the use of the assessed contributions budget and has since extended the mandate and the terms of the mission beyond a strict six months. Nonetheless, participants agreed that UNSOA has not always met the needs of the mission. The AMISOM-UNSOA relationship is hindered by two rather large bureaucracies. As one participant put it, 'AMISOM is out there fighting and dying for the mandate.' A problem with UN's well-established peace operation culture is that, 'counterinsurgency operations are different from regular peacekeeping.' The UN 'is not flexible enough ... to meet combat reality like that in Somalia. It cannot supply lethal ammunition.' Water and fuel are also too low to enable troops to be effective in battle. The UNSC allowed for 12,000 uniformed troops for AMISOM, but made no mention of the civilian components. In practice, the mission has had to move towards having a civilian component.

AUPSC and strategy

One positive development is that the AUPSC provides more strategic guidance to AMISOM than it tended to do during previous missions. This is probably because AUPSC feels a higher sense of ownership of AMISOM than of UNAMID. The group still thought that AUPSC could improve in this respect. Knowledge and engagement still rests with a few individuals: 'We have come a long way since AMIS but strategic thinking for AMISOM rests more on the shoulders of a handful of officers and the commissioner. Member states are not involved enough in oversight. Mandate renewal happens in an *ad hoc* manner.'

AUPSC has maintained throughout that Somalia is a global issue needing more international attention and support. At one point, AUPSC debated whether AMISOM needed a peace-enforcement mandate. Uganda wanted this, but the AUPSC was not of one mind and ultimately did not upgrade the mission, since the UNSC and donors had not pledged the necessary logistical and lethal equipment.

AMISOM's mandate

The support challenges are due partly to the gap between the mandate and the actual character of the mission. Participants debated whether AMISOM was best described as a peace operation or a peace enforcement or a Chapter VIII enforcement mission. As one participant commented: 'We are dealing with so many issues: terrorism, state-building, peacekeeping, post conflict reconstruction, peacemaking.' The AU's limited support staff have to manage both the mission (with the lack of clarity about its basis) and several coexisting support models. The time and energy required to do this is significant, and sometimes the AMISOM mission has had to refuse offers of support because it cannot absorb, maximise and account for them. One participant noted: 'There is a good management and finance division, but there are problems of transparency and dealing with the volume of work.' At the mission level in Nairobi, the staff are too few and there has been no finance team. The mission cannot manage or absorb the bilateral funds being offered. For example, a Spanish contribution of $1.8 million for humanitarian work could not be used and was returned. The challenge with coexisting models is not always lack of funds. Sometimes it is the inability of the mission to maximise the support arrangements that are there. There has been a lack of dedicated support staff in AMISOM, as well as at AUHQ.

The AU needs to clarify what mission support capacity it wants AMISOM to have. Does the AU want to limit itself to liaison or should it have its own mission support capacity? Currently, UN support is designed as a standard Chapter VI peacekeeping operation, but on the ground AMISOM is engaged in a Chapter VII-type robust operation, somewhere between peace enforcement and war.

Another question raised was the degree to which AMISOM should be a multidimensional operation. 'Does the UN want to support a military mission in Mogadishu, or a multidimensional peace operation? If the latter, then AMISOM needs more support for its civilian police and civilian component.' 'How much civilian capacity does AMISOM need (political affairs, humanitarian liaison, communications) when you have the UN political mission and UN agencies fulfilling some of these roles?' AMISOM does not necessarily need civilian capacity at the same level as a typical multidimensional UN operation. But a participant remarked that AMISOM needs its own dedicated political affairs capacity and that it should at least have the capacity to liaise among the mission, UN agencies and others that are providing these civilian roles. At present, however, AMISOM's small civilian component is not included in the UN logistical support package.

High Casualty Rate

One of the most tragic challenges facing AMISOM is the high casualty rate. One participant said that more troops have been lost in AMISOM than in the 50 years of UN peacekeeping. Many contributory factors were mentioned, such as the intensity of the conflict, the insurgents' tactics and the terrain. From a support perspective, several factors were mentioned, including poor command and control mechanisms, insufficient training, inappropriate equipment and poor intelligence.

'Ad-hocery'

Gadin explains that the support for AMISOM has three pillars: institutional capacity building and technical advice by the UN to AU to plan, deploy and manage AMISOM; provision and delivery of logistical support to AMISOM by the UN; and voluntary financial and in-kind support to the AU and TCCs to AMISOM by bilateral partners and institutions. There are two financing systems: an assured financial system, which is the assessed budget of the UN, and an unpredictable, voluntary financial system. This was not the result of deliberate strategy, but has come about in an *ad hoc* organic fashion. AMISOM is performing a critically important role on behalf of the international community ('AMISOM is there doing what international and regional peace and security demands'), but the support it receives does not seem to reflect this role.

Capacity building

The lack of predictable funding and other resources is a major obstacle to medium- to long-term planning. As a result, 'we risk ending up with capacity substitution and not capacity building.' The support package has resulted in significant improvements in AMISOM's operation. The mission needs catering, furniture, welfare. A guaranteed, sustainable and predictable funding mechanism is needed, argues Gadin in his chapter. More can be done, he continues, particularly if the UNSC mandates that the core needs of the mission must be met. But these needs have been left to voluntary contributions. As one person commented, the trust fund is a good idea, but leaving funding of core needs to voluntary contributions is inadequate. 'When contributions are made to the trust fund there are caveats on how the money can be used. It boils down to what these partners want to provide and what interests they have at play. This needs to be resolved at the strategic level.'

Another view was that there has been organisational learning from AMIS, UNAMID, AMISOM. We would be less harsh on ourselves if we weighed the hard realities that forced us into these situations. Peace operations are successful to the extent they lower the casualties and surpass non-intervention. Success should be based on what was avoided rather than on ideals (the protection of civilians is one such ideal).

The AUHQ has to date lacked a mission support capacity like the UN's DFS, but this is now being developed. 'We are getting better at institutionalising knowledge but we still reinvent the wheel at so many levels.' Troops have learned skills (storage, management, air support, etc.) but there is little knowledge increment in the mission. Training has to be given every year because of the rotation of troops, and one view was that 'we should keep troops a minimum of 18–24 months.'

Ownership

The memorandum of understanding between AMISOM and UNSOA on implementation needs to be reviewed and revised. It spells out a coordination mechanism that identifies the head of mission [spell out] as the AU coordinator and the UNSOA director as UN coordinator. However, there have been a few instances when communication and coordination between AMISOM and UNSOA did not originate with or involve the official coordinators, thus creating problems. In the period when there was insufficient civilian management in AMISOM (for instance, when the chief administrative officer post was vacant), UNSOA had no choice but to engage force headquarters directly. A further complicating factor has been when the TCCs have been engaged directly by UNSOA without the necessary involvement of AUPSOD or AMISOM.

UNSOA delivery aspects

UNSOA is an implementing agency. The problem lies with the mandating authority that sets out the policy directives and the Secretariat, which outlines the operational guidelines. There needs to be enhanced engagement between the UN Secretariat and AU Commission on one hand and UNSC and AUPSC on the other, especially for the purposes of shared/joint analysis. Beyond transmission of decisions, there is a need for prior discussion on the rationale for such decisions in order to gauge UNSC's appetite to endorse and authorise the support required for the implementation of such decisions.

To conclude, the AMISOM session made a strong call for greater UN flexibility in delivering the support package. Neither the AU nor UN can go on, Gadin argues, doing things in the way they are used to. A comprehensive support package is required that guarantees resources to the AU in a predictable and sustainable manner such that it has sufficient capacity to meet the real challenges. This can only be assured through the UN assessed contributions budget. The UNSC has 'stressed the importance of predictable, reliable and timely resources' for AMISOM and called on the international community to provide more support for the force. However, the P5 are still cautious about expanding the use of UN assessed contributions to support AMISOM, or any proposal that would significantly increase the financial burden on member states.

The necessity for a shared strategic vision between the AU, the UN and relevant stakeholders has been emphasised throughout this report. As we saw, lack of systematic strategic thinking has adverse implications for the strength of the international consensus, the sustainability of funding mechanisms and the effectiveness of AU-UN synergies. The next section expands on the role of the AU and on funding models.

Strategic vision and the Role of the AU

The lack of strategic thinking among all the stakeholders is weakening international consensus with negative implications on the ground. During the seminar, discussions of strategic visions and consensus often came back to the role and capacity of the AU. Participants time and again mentioned that one of the major obstacles to a shared strategic vision is the inability of the AU to muster the resources and capacity to play its role on the African continent.

In fact, the AU also needs to clarify the role it wants to play in the international arena. Overall, four problems were highlighted: the lack of AU strategic thinking; the lack of AU unity; the role of AU member states; and the relationship between the AU and RECs. In the debate over hybrid models, the lack of a clear vision regarding the role of the AU is hampering development of effective solutions. A recent report notes that the AU sees hybrid peace operations and other innovative approaches to peacekeeping, peacemaking and peacebuilding as the way of the future, 'as the strength of such joint ventures draws from the universal character of the UN and the advantages embedded in regionalism' (AU 2012 §105).[5]

Nevertheless, seminar participants emphasised that for the AU to advocate any type of hybrid mission, it must first have a clear view of its overall peace and security strategy. Developing a support model without such a vision would be like 'putting the cart before the horse.' How can one build a partnership and move forward without understanding the strategic objectives of the AU as a peace and security actor in the region. In this context, one participant explained during the final discussion that:

> The AU needs to focus and prioritise. What we need is a paradigm shift in getting involved in a conflict. Troops are expensive so we need to look at tools for prevention and mediation. The OAU has a very good track record for mediation but it is not sexy and rarely publicised. Why did we abandon it? There is a need for mediation in Africa. The AUPSC must understand its role, mission and events on the ground. The AUPSC probably does not know how many casualties there were last week in AMISOM. It does not register. Teams from NYC and the EU ask detail stuff and know much more [than the AUPSC].

In this context, there is a need for greater commitment and unity within the AU. The AU needs to discuss its political role and clarify the kind of peace and security actor it wants to be.

> We are building an institution with good offices, mediation, council of the wise, etc. but do we fully appreciate the comparative advantage of the AU as a peace and security actor in the region. How can we leverage the role the AU should play compared to other actors?

Many participants agreed these questions need to be answered. Only once the role of the AU has been decided can capacity begin to be built. Indeed, the issue of conceptual clarity is crucial since it must precede decisions about what capacity is most needed: 'What are we training people for? Peacekeeping or multidimensional peace operations? Today we train for multidimensional operations, so states must think about the importance of these missions and reassess their commitments.'

---

5   The report also states that experience had demonstrated that support using UN assessed contributions was the most viable response to the challenge at hand, especially when the operations are undertaken with UNSC consent. Support packages should be in line with the UNSC's global mandate (AU 2012 §110).

Discussion of the role of the AU must take into account the political reality and the influence of powerful states. For example, over the last decades, non-compliance and free-riding among member states have constrained the organisation, especially its international standing. There is a political dimension to the AU and state collaboration goes beyond isolated peace operations. When Sudan does not allow in needed equipment (such as armoured personnel carriers) this is not a technical issue specific to one peace operation, it is a matter of AU members not complying with AU principles and rules. One obstacle is the lack of mechanism to ensure cooperation and implementation of principles. Non-compliance is not met with sanctions. Another issue is the need to place political principles above political expediency. The AU did not want to disagree with Libya regarding the location of the peace process in Sirte, and this proved counterproductive for the Darfur peace talks. These political issues are at the heart of the AU, and what is certain is that 'the AUPSC and UNSC will need to think of whose political agenda they help advance with their decisions.'

Besides powerful AU states, it is necessary to consider the political influence of the host state. In this regard, the case of Darfur is telling. The government of Sudan consistently undermined the ability of AMIS and UNAMID to carry out their mandates by obstructing their operations and placing limitations on their freedom of movement.

Finally, we turn to the relationship between the AU and RECs. Tied to the question of the AU's role is the question of what comparative advantages the AU has vis-à-vis the RECs. For the AU, it is problematic that it must compete with sub-regional organisations for funding: sometimes, AU member states are more inclined to fund sub-regional actors than the AU. For example, up to 17 December 2011 Rwanda has paid $8 million to the East African Community but less than $2 million to the AU. One participant was prompted to ask: 'Is it not time that we reconsider criteria to assess the contribution of AU member states? Is it not time for the AU to say, when it looks for resources, that maybe it should rely on other regional organisations like ECOWAS?' These issues are fraught with difficulty, since RECs are often more politicised and their effectiveness in peace and security matters is thereby curtailed. Overall, more discussion is certainly needed on how to coordinate and harmonise the strategic relationships between the AU, RECs and the UN.

Funding Models

Support models are often based on original and *ad hoc* funding mechanisms that draw on voluntary contributions from states and international organisations. In AMIS, UNAMID and AMISOM, the funding models are different but general issues have emerged. In discussing support models, funding is often said to be the key problem, but seminar participants time and again explained that funding is only one issue among many. Various factors make funding a challenge, including predictability, sustainability, the lack of working capital, independence and conditionalities. These are briefly discussed in turn.

Most funding for peace operations in Africa comes from Western donors and in this regard two divergent views were expressed by seminar participants. One was that African governments who request predictable funding for AU peace operations from the UNSC 'need to put their money where their mouth is'. The problem is that African states are asking for external funding but this must go hand in hand with member states taking the AU's role more seriously. The need is also to close the gap between money pledged and money delivered and for future budgets to be in line with hopes, expectations and official discourse. A strong commitment by African states is all the more relevant given the current geopolitical and economic context, with Western donors facing a debt crisis and North African countries no longer able to play a leading role at the AU. One seminar participant posed the following question: 'Will the AU as a political project be viable, with funding no longer flowing from North African countries?'

Some participants suggested that AU member states should be investing in the peace and security structure through assessed contributions and through voluntary contributions to the African Peace Fund. One perspective on funding and world economic context was that in harsh times, all donors are going to reflect on priorities and results. Donors and the AU's partners will ask what the funding pattern of AU member states is telling us? Does it work? The development of the ASF is more donor-driven than AU member state-driven and this will be a growing concern for donors. This situation heightens the need for the AU to become more comfortable with internal criticism: 'We have to be honest with our partners.'

The recession and the need to find new funding avenues could provide an opportunity to reconsider donor relations and demands from the AU. Indeed, the 'AU, UN and EU do not see the situation in the same way and do not identify the same needs when it comes to intervention.' It is ultimately the UNSC that decides which resolution will pass, and the AU side have the feeling that UNSC resolutions are often not comprehensive enough and do not reflect the specific challenges in a conflict and mission area. Another issue noted by some participants is that donors do not always align support with building AU capacity but are more intent on showing their domestic audiences what they are doing in the name of peace.

Western-funded training and equipment sometimes creates more conflict when it is not commensurate with needs. All support models have caveats about and conditionalities on how the money can be used. 'It boils down to what these partners want to provide and what interests they have at play.' One potential solution would be to create the conditions to foster a shared agenda. The UNSC, UN Secretariat, AUPSC would need to meet regularly to clarify the strategic needs for peacekeeping and to determine what structure must be put in place that is appropriate to the mandate and the evolving situation.

The EU has been one of APSA's keenest funders and the AU needs to value this long-term strategic partner and its willingness to support 'African-driven and-owned approaches'. It is of concern to the AU that the EU 'worries that the AU does not have working capital to bridge gaps in donor support. If we look at funding requirements for the next year the EU will have concerns. How to continue support?' One proposal was to, 'set up working groups and brainstorm on pragmatic issues together with governance experts and finance experts on how to finance and manage the peace fund'. In Somalia, the EU supported AMISOM from day one with a mission allowance for peacekeepers. More than €250 million has been spent overall on mission allowances alone, €12-15 million per month in total. In additon, 'European officers have trained Somalis in Uganda, launched the first naval operation ATALANTA, have protected transport coming into Somalia and have been combating piracy.'

The relationship between the AU and UN is different and other issues have emerged. During the seminar, there was a feeling that the relationship needed to evolve and one participant declared that 'the UN and the AU cannot become two organisations doing the same thing. There must be synergies and officials must meet often, effectively and with less anger.' Participants held that the UNSC's conversations regarding automatic funding for AUPSC decisions had stalled. 'There will not be anything that will make the UNSC lose political control. But we need to discuss different means of funding.'

The issue of funding is often tied to broader issues of political commitment, trust and national power struggles. As such, 'we need to recognise that not all the stakeholders involved are committed to make operations work as best ... they can.' Funding models are also diminishing the independence of the AU: as long as the AU depends on funds from outside, it is not free.[6] This is as true of long-term funding for APSA as of funding for individual peace

---

6   The AU Commission chairperson argued in his report that member states need to shoulder their responsibilities fully in this respect by providing increased resources and thereby enhancing ownership of African peace initiatives (AU 2012 §114).

operations. Without support structures, the AU cannot effectively lead or own peace operations, but current AU initiatives are too vulnerable to external pressures and demands.

Transparency is also high on the list of donor demands. On this topic, 'one idea is to have an AU Peace Fund board of directors to manage the peace fund independently.' This might encourage partners to put money in the fund. Ultimately all donors and stakeholders should realise that their interests are to a large extent interdependent and that the credibility of the UNSC in Africa as well as the emerging AU role are at stake in the discussions of the strengths and weaknesses of support models. AMISOM is a good example, since Somalia is a global issue, and yet the UNSC allows a peace enforcement-like mission to 'go around begging for funding'. This impacts the legitimacy not only of the AU but also of the international peace and security architecture.

Between *ad hoc* planning and straightjackets

The support models have not been the result of long-term and careful planning. Rather, they have tended to arise from the need to find solutions to complex situations. The different support models that have been implemented now form part of the peacekeeping toolbox. There is no one model suitable for all situations and the different models should not be used as straightjackets. Support strategies must be holistic and flexible and models need to be adequate, early, predictable and institutionalised. In any event, flexibility does not mean complete *ad hoc*ery. Models need to be sufficiently flexible and politically viable as well as suited to the diversity of mission types and conflicts in Africa. For example, a model requiring great harmonisation and cooperation may not be suitable in volatile situations and ongoing wars. Likewise, the direct donor support model is appropriate for small-scale operations and for the early stages of an operation, when the UN is not yet able to provide support or before it takes over a mission. In Sudan, jointness undermines efforts at times but the partnership remains a strength. Jointness may work in some cases but in a fast changing political context can be perceived as a failing. The greatest difficulty with jointness lies at the political level, not the operational. Within AUPSC, too few member states are involved in reporting or oversight, as if they have no stake in the conflicts in which the AU intervenes. Moreover, mandate renewal happens in an *ad hoc* manner.

In a context where flexibility is central to the success of peace operations and yet where *ad hoc* planning has proven inadequate, an alternative must be found. Some sort of institutionalisation to ensure that lessons are learnt and collaboration is effective is required, but this is by no means a call for acceptance of constraining models that would become straightjackets. Middle ground must be found. One path is to begin an in-depth discussion on systems, processes and models. Dependable systems as well as cooperation mechanisms that can be drawn on to implement solutions adapted to the situation on the ground are needed.

Conclusion

Over the last decades, the UN has strengthened its collaboration with regional organisations to maintain peace and security in Africa. As part of this relationship, different support models have been implemented with varying degrees of success. UN member states benefit from better enabling their strategic security partner, the AU, to do a more efficient job: they fulfil their duties and are less open to criticism that they are neglecting international peace and security in Africa. Despite its limitations, this cooperation between the UN and African regional actors has become the *sine qua non* for successful conflict management on the continent. In this context, it is interesting to consider whether past and present experiences with support models will lead to a shared strategic vision and new policies on peace operations, or whether they will only harden the positions of the AU and UN on leadership, principles, funding and organisational culture as applied to Africa. Collaboration is necessary, but as Banseka wonders:

> ...whose *modus operandi* takes precedence and why? What are the determinants of success offered by both organisations? What is their level of experience in peacekeeping and peacemaking? What is their understanding of and empathy for local realities that will ensure success? Does the mere ability to fund these activities make a difference?

This seminar on support models is a first step in considering the various issues arising from jointness and hybridity. Overall, there is a feeling that today people are more frank and honest about what the AU-UN partnership issues are. Seminar participants identified the following core issues: capacity building of the AU Commission; increasing political commitment by African member states; longer-term support relationships between the AU and partners, and; the reassessment by UNSC permanent members of the potential of a stronger AU-UN partnership. Continuing the debate on these issues is critical, even if the AU's political and peace and security departments are reluctant to make space for these reflections.

This report has identified specific tensions between the AU and UN arising from joint missions. While there is no easy solution to all of these issues, providing an explicit outline of these tensions is a first step. What is certain is that AU-UN collaboration needs to be strengthened. Both organisations need a relationship that is at once flexible and institutionalised. Dependable systems need to exist to guide the two in responding to issues that arise at short notice. On this matter, the systems, procedures, processes that should be part of the 'toolbox' of support models appropriate for the future must be discussed. Both organisations need to invest more in the relationship, especially when it comes to the interconnected issues of shared strategy, capacity building, funding, and the like.

Bibliography

Aboagye, F.B., *ECOMOG: A Sub-regional experience in Conflict Resolution, Management and Peacekeeping in Liberia*, Accra: Sedco, 1999.

Adebajo, Adekeye, 'The Security Council and Three Wars in Western Africa', in Vaughan Lowe, Adam Roberts, Jennifer Welsh and Dominik Zaum (eds), *The United Nations Security Council and War*, 466–93, Oxford: Oxford University Press, 2008.

Adebajo, Adekeye, *Building peace in West Africa: Liberia, Sierra Leone, and Guinea-Bissau*, London: Lynne Rienner, 2002.

Adebajo, Adekeye and Chris Landsberg, 'Back to the future: UN peacekeeping in Africa', *International Peacekeeping* 7, no. 4 (2000): 161–88.

Adibe, Clement E., 'The Liberian conflict and the ECOWAS-UN partnership', *Third World Quarterly* 18, no. 3 (1997): 471–88.

African Union (AU), '*UN-AU Partnership on Peace and Security: Towards Greater Strategic Political Coherence*', Draft Report, Validation Workshop on AU-UN Strategic Partnership, Addis Ababa, Ethiopia, 3 May 2011.

AU, 'Protocol relating to the establishment of the Peace and Security Council of the AU', 2002.

AU Peace and Security Council 307th meeting, Report of the Chairperson of the Commission on the Partnership between the African Union and the United Nations on peace and security: Towards greater strategic and political coherence, PSC/PR/2.(CCCVII) 9 January 2012.

AU Peace and Security Council 17th Meeting, Report by the Chairperson of the AU Commission, PSC/PR/2(XVII), 20 October 2004.

African Union, *Roadmap for the operationalization of the African Standby Force*. Experts' meeting on the relationship between the AU and the Regional Mechanisms for Conflict Prevention, Management and Resolution, Addis Ababa, 22-23 March 2005, EXP/AU-RECS/ASF/4(i).

AU Executive Council, '*The Common African Position on the Proposed Reform of the United Nations: "The Ezulwini Consensus"*', 7th Extraordinary Session, Ext/EX.CL/2(vii), 7–8 March 2005.

African Union Executive Council, 18th Ordinary Session, 'Decision on the Contributions of Member States', EX.CL/Dec.418 (XIII), Doc. PRC/Rpt. (XVI) 1, 2008.

Aning, Kwesi, *International Dimensions of Internal Conflict: The Case of Liberia and West Africa*, Copenhagen: Centre for Development Research, 1997.

Aning, Kwesi, 'The UN and the African Union's security architecture: Defining an emerging partnership?', *Critical Currents*, no. 5 (2008): 9–24.

Annan, Kofi, Report of the Secretary-General to the General Assembly and the Security Council. *'The Causes of Conflict and the Promotion of Durable Peace and Sustainable Development in Africa'*, A/52/871-S/1998/318, 13 April 1998.

Bellamy, Alex J. and Paul Williams, 'Who's Keeping the peace? Regionalization and Contemporary Peace Operations', *International Security* 29, no. 4 (2005): 157–95.

Berman, Eric G., 'The Security Council's Reliance on Burden-Sharing: Collaboration or Abrogation?', *International Peacekeeping* 4, no. 1 (1998): 1 –21.

Berman, Eric G. and Katie E. Sams, Peacekeeping in Africa: Capabilities and Culpabilities, Geneva: UNIDIR, 2000.

Boulden, Jane (ed.), *Dealing With Conflict in Africa: The United Nations and Regional Organizations*, New York: Palgrave Macmillan, 2003.

Carey, Margaret, 'Peacekeeping in Africa: Recent Evolution and Prospects', in Oliver Furley and Roy May (eds), *Peacekeeping in Africa*, 13 –27, Aldershot: Ashgate, 1998.

Clapham, Christopher, 'The United Nations and Peacekeeping in Africa', ISS Monograph no. 36 (1999).

Cleaver, Gerry and Roy May, 'Peace keeping: The African Dimension', *Review of African Political Economy* 22, no. 66 (1995): 485 –97.

Coleman, Katharina P., *International Organisations and Peace Enforcement: The Politics of International Legitimacy*, Cambridge: Cambridge University Press, 2007.

de Coning, Cedric, 'The Evolution of Peace Operations in Africa: Trajectories and Trends', *Journal of International Peacekeeping* 14, nos 1–2 (February 2010a): 6 –26.

de Coning, Cedric, 'The future of Peacekeeping in Africa', *Conflict Trends* 3 (2006).

de Coning, Cedric, 'The Emerging UN/AU Peacekeeping Partnership', *Conflict Trends* I (2010b).

de Coning, Cedric, 'Peace Operations in Africa: The Next Decade', *NUPI Working Paper* 721, 2007.

de Coning, Cedric and Yvonne Kasumba (eds), *The Civilian Dimension of the African Standby Force*, Durban: African Union and ACCORD, 2010.

De Coning, Cedric and Walter Lotze, 'Looking Back When Looking Forward: Peacebuilding Policy Approaches and Processes in Africa', *Journal of Peacebuilding and Development* 5, no. 2 (2010):. 107 –12.

Diarra, Boubacar G., 'Civilian protection key to AMISOM operations', *New Vision,* 12 July 2011.

Downie, R., 'Qaddafi's Tangled Legacy in Africa', *Centre for Strategic and International Studies,* 2 March 2011.

ECOWAS, Decision A/DEC.2/11/90, Relating to the Adoption of an ECOWAS Peace Plan for Liberia and the Entire West African Sub-Region, 1990.

EU Council, Secretariat Factsheet: EU Engagement in Somalia, EU/Somalia 07, February 2010.

Franke, Benedikt, 'In Defense of Regional Peace Operations in Africa', *Journal of Humanitarian Assistance*, February (2006): 1–14.

Furley, Oliver and Roy May, *Peacekeeping in Africa*, Aldershot: Ashgate, 1998.

Gelot, Linnéa, *Legitimacy, Peace Operations and Global-Regional Security: The African Union-United Nations Partnership in Darfur*, London: Routledge 2012.

Goulding, Marrack, 'The United Nations and Conflict in Africa since the Cold War', *African Affairs* 98, no. 391 (1999): 155 –66.

Gowan, Richard and Jake Sherman, *Peace Operations Partnerships: Complex but Necessary Cooperation,* Center for International Peace Operations, March 2012.

Hentz, James, Frederik Söderbaum and Rodrigo Tavares, 'Regional Organisations and African Security: Moving the Debate Forward', *African Security* 2, no. 2/3 (2009): 206 –17.

Herbst, Jeffrey, 'African Peacekeepers and State Failure', in Robert Rotberg (ed.), *Peacekeeping and Peace Enforcement in Africa: Methods of Conflict Prevention,* 16 –33, Washington DC: Brookings Institution Press, 2000.

Herbst, Jeffrey, 'Crafting Regional Cooperation in Africa', in Amitav Acharya and Alastair I. Johnston (eds), *Crafting Cooperation: Regional International Institutions in Comparative Perspective,* 129 –44, Cambridge: Cambridge University Press, 2007.

Holt V.K. and T.C. Berkman, ' *The Impossible Mandate? Military Preparedness, the Responsibility to Protect and Modern Peace Operations,* Washington: Henry L. Stimson Center, 2006.

Human Rights Watch, 'Darfur Bleeds: Recent Cross-Border Violence in Chad', February 2006.

Hutchful, E., The ECOMOG Experience with Peacekeeping in West Africa, Monograph No 36: Whither Peacekeeping in Africa? 1999.

Fleshman, Michael, 'Darfur: An Experiment in African Peacekeeping. Is African Union-UN hybrid a model for the future?', *Africa Renewal,* December 2010.

Graham, Kennedy and Tania Felicio, *Regional Security and Global Governance,* Brussels: VUB University Press, 2006.

International Crisis Group, 'A study for comprehensive peace in Sudan', *Africa Report* no. 130, 26 July 2007.

International Peace Academy, 'The AU in Sudan: Lessons for the African Standby Force', March 2007.

Malan, Mark, 'The OAU and African Subregional Organisations: A closer look at the "peace pyramid"', ISS Occasional Paper no. 36 (1999).

Murithi, Timothy, 'The African Union's Evolving Role in Peace Operations', *African Security Review* 17, no. 1 (2008): 70 –82.

Nhlapo, W., 'Peacebuilding in Burundi', paper presented at the CCR/FES seminar on African Perspectives on the UN Peacebuilding Commission, Maputo, Mozambique, 3 –4 August 2006.

Onoja, A., 'Peacekeeping Challenges in Africa: The Darfur Conflict', African Centre for the Constructive Resolution of Disputes, *Conflict Trends,* 2008.

Romano Prodi, 'G-8 focuses on continent: Peacekeeping stressed as key to development success', *Washington Times,* 8 July 2009.

UN General Assembly, Approved Resources for Peacekeeping Operations for the Period 1 July 2011 to 30 June 2012, 65th Session, Fifth Committee, 22 July 2011.

UN General Assembly, 62nd General Assembly Fifth Committee Meeting, GA/AB/3828, Fifth Committee, 19th meeting, 19 November 2007.

UN doc. Charter of the United Nations, Chapter VIII, Article 52(1) Francisco, 26 June 1945.

UN Department of Peacekeeping Operations (UNPDKO), Fact Sheet, 31 March 2012, http://www.un.org/en/peacekeeping/resources/statistics/factsheet.shtml

UNDPKO, UNAMID Facts and Figures: African Union-United Nations Hybrid Operation in Darfur, 29 July 2011.

UNPDKO, *A New Partnership Agenda: Charting a New Horizon for UN Peacekeeping,* DPKO and DFS, New York, July 2009.

UN General Assembly and Security Council (UNGA-UNSC) doc., Report of the Panel on United Nations Peace Operations (Brahimi Report). Identical letters dated 21 August 2000 from the Secretary-General to the President of the General Assembly and the President of the Security Council, A/55/305–S/2000/809, 21 August 2000.

UNGA-UNSC doc., Identical letters dated 24 December 2008 from the Secretary-General addressed to the President of the General Assembly and the President of the Security Council (Prodi Report), A/63/666 –S/2008/813, 31 December 2008.

UN Peacekeeping Best Practices Unit, 'Lessons learned Study on the Start-up Phase of the United Nations Mission in Liberia', Peacekeeping Best Practices Unit, April 2004.

UN Security Council (UNSC), Resolution 1503, New York, S/RES/1503, 28 August 2003.

UNSC, Security Council Resolution 1556, S/RES/1556, 30 July 2004.

UNSC, Resolution 1769, New York, S/RES/1769, 31 July 2007.

UNSC, Resolution 2033, New York, S/RES/2033, 28 January 2012a.

UNSC, Resolution 2036, New York, S/RES/2036, 22 February 2012b.

Vogt, Margaret Aderinsola, 'Co-operation between the United Nations and the OAU in the Management of African Conflicts', ISS Monograph no. 36 (1999).

Williams, Paul D., 'The Peace and Security Council of the African Union: Evaluating an embryonic international institution.' *Journal of Modern African Studies* 47, no. 4 (2009): 603 –26.

Interview

Monie Captan, Monrovia, Liberia, 5 July 2011. He is currently an associate professor, University of Liberia and was formerly Liberian foreign minister in Charles Taylor's regime.

Notes on Contributors

Mustapha Abdallah is a research fellow with the International Institutions Programme (IIP), at the research department, Kofi Annan International Peacekeeping Training Centre. Focusing on institutions such as the AU and ECOWAS, he undertakes research in mediation, peacekeeping and conflict resolution and also supports the programme for the implementation of the ECOWAS conflict prevention framework adopted in 2008. He holds a Master's degree in international affairs from the University of Ghana, Legon.

General (rtd.) Martin L. Agwai was a career military officer and one of the longest-serving officers in the Nigerian Armed Forces. General Agwai was the last force commander of AMIS in 2007 and the first force commander of UNAMID, from December 2007 to August 2009. In 2002, General Agwai was seconded to UN headquarters in New York as deputy military advisor in the DPKO. Nigerian President Chief Olusegun Obasanjo appointed him as chief of army staff in 2003. His achievements in leading the Nigerian army earned him a promotion to four-star general and his appointment as chief of defence staff in 2006. In 2003 he was appointed a Commander of the Order of the Federal Republic (CFR), while in 2010 the Africa Centre of Strategic Studies awarded him the 2010 Visionary Award for his achievements in peace and security in Africa.

Dr Kwesi Aning is currently director of the graduate studies and research department of the Kofi Annan International Peacekeeping Training Centre in Accra. Until January 2008, he served as a senior consultant to the UN Department of Political Affairs and wrote a UN Secretary-General's report on the relationship between the UN and regional organisations, particularly the AU, on peace and security, which has been submitted to the UNSC. He is a non-resident fellow at the Center on International Cooperation, New York University.

Maj. Gen. (rtd.) Henry Anyidoho is the former deputy special representative of the Secretary-General, UNAMID (31 Dec 2007-12 June 2010). He played an instrumental role in transforming AMIS into UNAMID, coordinating, for instance, the UN light and heavy support packages to the AU Mission in Sudan 2006-2007. He was also the joint chief of staff of the AU Darfur integrated task force, May 2005–Nov 2006. His most recent position in UN peacekeeping before retiring was as deputy force commander and chief of staff of the UN Assistance Mission for Rwanda. After that he was posted to the Ghanaian ministry of defence as special assistant to the defence minister. He was promoted to the rank of major-general in 2000 and was decorated with the Distinguished Service Order for gallantry. He retired in 2001 after almost 41 years of active service. He was awarded the Order of the Volta and has authored *Guns over Kigali* (1997) and his autobiography *My Journey ... Every Step* (2010). He is a senior research associate at King's College, London.

Sivuyile Bam has since 2008 been the head of the Peace Support Operations Division in the Peace and Security Department of the African Union Commission. He has been seconded by the South African department of defence, which he joined in 1997, and where, prior to his current appointment, he served as the director of research and analysis in the defence secretariat. His duties included research into the AU and SADC, African multilateral institutions the department of defence was participating in. He was part of the South African government delegation in discussions to set up the African Standby Force and develop other security-related policies such as the Solemn Declaration on the Common African Defence and Security Policy, the AU Non-Aggression and Common Defence Pact and the SADC Non-Aggression Pact. He holds a BA (Hons) degree in political studies from the University of South Africa.

Prof. Cage Banseka is currently a political affairs officer and deputy chief of staff with the AU-UN joint mediation support team for Darfur. He was previously a political affairs officer with the AU and worked in Sudan. He teaches conflict resolution at the Protestant University of Central Africa and prior to that at the University of Muenster, Germany. He has several publications on peace and security and practical conflict resolution, with a focus on sub-Saharan Africa.

Cedric de Coning is a research fellow at the African Centre for the Constructive Resolution of Disputes (ACCORD) and NUPI, and a special advisor to the head of the AU's Peace Support Operations Division. He has served as a South African diplomat in Washington DC and Addis Ababa; as an election observer with the AU in Ethiopia, Sudan and Algeria; and as a civilian peacekeeper with the UN in Timor Leste and in New York. He is a PhD candidate at the University of Stellenbosch. His research interests include interventions (how transformative should they be?), peacekeeping and peacebuilding (linkages, trends and challenges), coherence (inherent contradictions and limits), civil-military coordination and civilian capacity. Theoretically, he is interested in the implications of complexity for international relations in general, and for peacekeeping and peacebuilding in particular. Recent publications include: 'Moving Beyond the Technical: Facing up to Peacebuilding's Inherent Contradictions', *African Security Review*, Vol. 20, Issue 1, March 2011, and 'Coherence and Coordination: The Limits of the Comprehensive Approach' (with Karsten Friis), *Journal of International Peacekeeping* 15, nos 1–2 (2011).

James Gadin is a political officer with AMISOM. He started out as a soldier in the Nigerian army, served in management in the multinational business sector, and then in civil society across West, East and Southern Africa in the areas of conflict management, peacebuilding and electoral assistance before joining the AU Commission. He holds a Master's degree in international affairs and diplomacy from Ahmadu Bello University, Zaria, Nigeria and certificates in negotiations and national and international security from John F. Kennedy School of Government, Harvard University.

Dr Linnéa Gelot is a researcher at NAI. She has also been a postdoctoral research fellow at the Gothenburg Centre of Globalisation and Development, University of Gothenburg, Sweden, since September 2010. Her primary specialisation is the relationship between Africa and the UN, and her book on this topic (*Legitimacy, Peace Operations and Global-Regional Security: The African Union-United Nations Partnership in Darfur*) has been published as part of Routledge's Security and Governance Series in 2012. She has also published on military interventions, the responsibility to protect and African politics in journals such as *Security Dialogue* and *African Affairs*.

Dr Ludwig Gelot is a senior lecturer in peace and development at the University of Gothenburg, Sweden, and consultant at the peacekeeping training programme of the UN Institute for Training and Research (UNITAR). He has taught development, peace and conflict resolution as well as specialist courses in Europe and Africa. He has recently developed rigorous and innovative courses on conflict analysis and conflict resolution for the peacekeeping training programme of UNITAR for military or civilian personnel in peace operations. He is currently researching the pre-deployment training needs of UN peacekeepers, the legitimacy of peace operations in Africa and sociopolitical transformations in the Middle East-North Africa region.

www.ingramcontent.com/pod-product-compliance
Lightning Source LLC
Chambersburg PA
CBHW070810280326
41934CB00012B/3142